From Debt To Prosperity
'Social Credit' Defined

Dave Robinson Institute
3 Linnell Circle
Brunswick, Maine 04011

dave-robinson-institute.com

From Debt To Prosperity

Social Credit is by no means a form of socialism. Social Credit is not a political party.

Social Credit is the best way to fight Socialism and Communism.

Social Credit wants to make every member of society a real capitalist, a shareholder in the wealth of the country.

This book is an adaptation of the book "From Debt To Prosperity" by J. Crate Larkin Published for the Louis Even Institute for Social Justice by —

The Pilgrims of Saint Michael
1101 Principale Street
Rougemont, QC
Canada - J0L 1M0

www.michaeljournal.org

For the U.S.A.
P.O. Box 86, South Deerfield, MA 01373

From Debt To Prosperity

From Debt To Prosperity

Contents

From Debt To Prosperity

PREFACE

Challenging the Bankers With 'Social Credit'
by Mark Anderson

AMERICAN FREE PRESS, September 6, 2010, ISSUE 36

The Pilgrims of Saint Michael held their 71st Social Credit Congress Sept. 4-6 at the Louis Even Institute near Montreal in Rougemont, Quebec, as this Catholic lay group continues to study and implement the sweeping monetary reform known as social credit. They are targeting the interest-bearing money system that is enslaving mankind.

This congress is among several events, ideas and movements that are taking root to battle the forces of economic and political oppression that have become highly visible to average citizens in recent years as a real depression settles upon us.

Not to be confused in any way with socialism, social credit is seen as perhaps the most promising way of returning the creation of money to sovereign hands — independent of private bankers — so money can come into existence without bearing interest. This would effectively end the "curse" of private, central bankers creating money that incurs mountainous, relentless interest charges that comprise the debts of nations.

For the second straight year, AMERICAN FREE PRESS has attended this congress, which also is attended by activists, religious leaders, former and current government officials and others from around the world.

Everyone in attendance remained gravely concerned about the extreme global control that central banks and crooked financial institutions exert upon us all, which has deepened poverty in the United States, Canada and the world.

This AFP editor has been studying social credit since September 2008, learning of it at the American Monetary Institute's annual fall conference in Chicago, Ill. There, Pilgrims Yves Jacques and Alain Pilote shared a profound book, *In this Age of Plenty,* by the late Louis Even. Even, a founder of the Pilgrim's headquarters, was a relentless advocate for dispossessed Canadians who lost their homes and livelihoods. He continued the teachings of social credit founder Clifford Hugh Douglas, A Scottish engineer.

Even's unshakable activism was in the 1960s. However, the economic situation is far worse today. So the social credit movement and others see a golden opportunity to turn the tide by teaching citizens how money is supposed to work, compared to the dysfunctional money system we have today.

Social credit essentially involves governments reclaiming the sovereign power of creating money interest-free in harmony with the nation's productive level.

On a parallel track, activists sympathies to the social credit movement, such as Mickey Paoletta of Pennsylvania and Bob Van Bemmelen of Michigan, and Mike Bower of Tennessee, are devising ways to help individual Americans and communities discover the road to freedom by escaping the debt system.

Paoletta, interviewed by AFP on Aug. 22, demonstrated a system to harness existing laws in order to use the court system and nullify credit card debts and other debts, and challenge mortgage foreclosures.

INTRODUCTION

National, Debt-Free Money

Chapter 1 from
Give Yourself Credit: Money Doesn't Grow On Trees

There is no reason for us to put up with recession, depression, and unemployment.

By using 2006 statistics, we can see that the U.S. Gross Domestic Product (GDP) came to about $14 trillion dollars, while the total income of the nation came to only about $10 trillion dollars, and at least 10% of that income was reinvested income rather than income spent on goods and services.

The total available purchasing power of the nation was only about $10 trillion dollars, or about $4 trillion dollars less than the total collective price of goods and services.

Where did consumers get the extra $4 trillion dollars? They had to borrow it from the banks that created it out of nothing with simple accounting entries on their books.

If the government were to replace this bank-created-out-of-nothing money with **national, debt-free money,** instead, the total money supply would remain unchanged and a whopping $4 trillion dollars in new *government issued* **national, debt-free money** would be fed into the economy without increasing the inflation rate, and this *government issued* **national, debt-free money** could be used to pay a guaranteed basic income for all Americans — such as $10,000 per adult and $5,000 per each dependent child — each year, — *instead of paying needless interest to the private, non-federal, Federal Reserve banks.*

If $4 trillion dollars of newly created, **national, debt-free money** were issued to fill the gap between GDP and our purchasing power, and this $4 trillion dollars of new, **national, debt-free money** were distributed among the people, the government would still have over $1 trillion dollars each year to satisfy its budgetary needs without a federal income tax.

By utilizing **national, debt-free money** Congress could stabilize prices, and output would increase to full employment.

There is no reason for us to put up with recession, depression and unemployment. The government simply has to put more money into circulation.

It can all be paid for if the government increased the money supply by issuing **national, debt-free money,** as Lincoln did at the start of the Civil War.

We suffer from a failure of consumer demand because of a lack of buying power — because of our failure to use our God-given **national credit** to prime the pump.

Our country was pulled out of the Depression by priming the pump with liquidity and funding new projects that put new money into the people's pocket.

Watering a liquidity starved economy with new, **national, debt-free money,** — instead of borrowing money at interest from the banks *and then giving it back to the banks* — would work wonders.

People want to work and there is work to be done.

Consumers want to purchase the fruits of their labor but they can't because of the anemic money supply. An infusion of new, **national, debt-free money** — instead of borrowing more interest laden debt from the banks — would get the wheels of production turning again.

Very little of borrowed money goes to improve infrastructure or to increase employment. Jobs are being out-sourced abroad while the public struggles to make the interest payments on the *needless federal debt* . . . and stay alive.

1
The National-Dividend

How to provide the necessities of life for the millions of unemployed, many of them eager to work, is perhaps the most urgent of our problems. Yet the need for their services in industry decreases daily.

All that is certain is that the number of workers required, however small today, is almost certain to decrease still further tomorrow. As the machine becomes more automatic, the number of machines that can be power-driven becomes limitless, and the quantity of power available from rivers, lakes, seas, and the sun itself, is limitless.

As machines replace men in man's struggle to abolish human drudgery it becomes more and more evident that what we have thought of as the "evil of unemployment" is but the natural result of our success in harnessing nature.

Science has so rapidly replaced **man-labor** with **machine-power** that today the amount of work necessary to keep everybody employed simply does not exist. Some of the best brains (scientists and others) have for 150 years or more been endeavoring to put the world out of work — and they have succeeded.

To take the attitude that everyone must work in order to live is simply to show oneself to be a remnant of the bygone days of scarcity.

The use of modern power-machinery is here to stay. Were we to throw away our scientific knowledge and the labor-saving devices it has produced, we would turn civilization back to barbarism. We have a problem, not so much of "un-*employ*-ment" as of "under-*empay*-ment" — lack of money and the inability to acquire it by working. The need is not to "make work" for the unemployed, but to devise some practical means to provide them with the buying-power they need to live.

The industrial machine is a lever, continuously being extended by progress, which enables the burdens of life to be lifted with ever-increasing ease. As the number of men required to work the lever decreases, the number set free to lengthen it increases.

The economic system exists to supply goods and services for consumption, and yet we make the mistake of thinking that it exists **to supply employment, instead of to supply goods**. Increasing abundance with a diminishing amount of human labor is possible for all. That is the reality we can no longer hide.

A new leisure, a forced freedom from the necessity to live by the sweat of our brow, is an inescapable by-product of modern science. We must accept this conclusion as fact and deal with it accordingly.

If we are to turn this new freedom, from a curse into a blessing, some practical means of supplying buying-power to the unemployed must be put into operation. The initial step in achieving economic security is to adopt a positive means, in addition to employment, to distribute buying-power to the nation's helpless and unemployed.

And we already have a working example of this method. In 1929, we all knew of people who lived on investment dividends — some of them still do — they are the not-employed. We do not call such people victims of unemployment — we call them instead fortunate persons of the leisure class.

But there is an economic difference between the man who lives on dividends and the man who has no job who can't buy food for his family. One man has the dividends that constitute buying-power and the other man does not.

It is an accepted business principle that the dividends of shareholders of a corporation come from the **appreciation** or increase in the net earning power of the value of investments.

To understand the practical background of a National-Dividend, such as Social Security or a negative income tax, we may well consider the United States to be the great business that it actually is, the UNITED STATES, INC., of which every individual consumer is a member holding stock. The business of this **association** is to produce wanted goods and distribute them for consumption.

In this **business association** every citizen of the UNITED STATES is a consuming shareholding partner in the total enterprise. The **association** exists for the benefit of each and every citizen and it has elected officers and directors represented by the Government.

From Debt To Prosperity

2
The Value Of Our Cultural Inheritance

The chief asset of this great **adventurous association**, the richest on the face of the earth, is its enormous power to produce wealth. This power is made possible principally by the sum total of our scientific knowledge such as chemistry, physics, engineering and the control over nature with which these sciences have endowed us. Our ability to produce wealth in abundance is perhaps four-fifths due mostly to the efficient organization of modern business intensified by the knowledge which centuries of discovery and research have given us.

This body of knowledge is the **Cultural Heritage** of the Nation under God. More and more in our daily life we depend upon this inheritance. Even in the last fifty years the findings of science have given us for everyday use energies and abilities undreamed of by our ancestors. The airplane and the radio are outstanding examples.

We do not ordinarily think much about our inherited power of control over the forces of nature. But our present standard of living is the fruit of the thought, scientific inventions, and labor, of many generations of men. The names of many of them are unknown to us now. In the production of any article today the discoveries of the past are equally as important as the efforts of those living today. These discoveries of the past belong to all of us; as a **Birthright-in-Fact**. The population of any country is the **Tenant-for-Life** of the culture.

Yet we carelessly take for granted the value of our culture. We use telephones, we drive automobiles over paved streets, and we live in steam-heated houses lighted by electricity. All of these are everyday experiences of our common Cultural Inheritance.

By virtue of our associating together and our joint participation in this knowledge, every citizen shares in the values of the nation's Cultural Inheritance. Every consumer is a joint beneficiary of the great national legacy of wealth.

As a shareholder in the Cultural Heritage of this rich nation, every American is entitled to receive National Dividends as his birthright. The fact of citizenship entitles each of us the right to share in the fruits of the total productive capacity of the corporate U.S.A.

Such dividends are the basic necessities of life: food, clothing, and shelter. The dividend represents our share in the increasing benefits of the power of production. As the machine displaces men, the wage-income previously paid to these men, must continue to be paid by the machines that displaced them. The dividend is thus the logical successor of the wage.

Under such conditions every individual would be possessed of purchasing-power which would be the reflection of his position as a "Tenant-for-Life" of the benefits of the Cultural Heritage handed down from generation to generation.

We have the wealth and the means to provide more of the benefits of life in abundance for all. But we lack the money to access our wealth. For the good of all, consumers must be enabled to consume. For when consumption is shut off by lack of buying-power, our wealth grows useless to everyone, producers and consumers alike.

A **National-Dividend** depends upon our increased ability to produce and deliver wealth. It is based directly upon an **appreciation** of the actual value of our Real-Wealth. On this solid foundation **National-Dividends** can be paid to every American citizen.

Let us outline briefly how such a Dividend would work in immediate operation.

Suppose, for example, that the first of every month, every American citizen, employed or unemployed, would receive a check that would supply his basic needs, signed by the Treasury of the United States, drawn against a **National Credit Account** and issued through an authorized bank, that would arrive by mail in a government envelope.

To visualize what would happen we have only to remember the miserable conditions of poverty everywhere evident in the world today. Millions now living on a bare subsistence level would at once satisfy long-suppressed needs and desires for goods. The Dividend-Check would be immediately cashed and the money used to buy needed goods.

This effective demand for goods would be felt first by retailers, then by wholesalers, and then by producers, resulting in millions of dollars worth of new business. We can hardly exaggerate the stimulus that this would give to business and industry in the form of confidence alone, to say nothing of the actual draft upon our unused productive capacities.

At first thought this example may perhaps seem extreme but in fact it is only a first timid step toward the Plenty that is now possible for all. Necessity, is driving us in this direction, and we cannot resist its pressure. Mounting taxes and growing debt wreck the efforts of business to produce and deliver wanted goods. The burden of increasing relief requirements financed by debt-money borrowed from the banking system is fast becoming as intolerable as it is hopelessly inadequate.

The most pressing needs of the moment could be met by means of what we call a **National-Dividend.** This would be provided by the creation of new money and its distribution as purchasing-power to the population as a whole, by exactly the same methods as are now used by the banking system to create new money today.

In its very first month a **National-Dividend** would accomplish much to revive business. It would gradually provide a rising standard of living for all American citizens, including the millions today who are struggling to keep body and soul together.

It must be clearly understood that increases in such a **National-Dividend** would depend directly upon increased production and consequent **appreciation** of Real-Wealth that would as a consequence occur. Beginning immediately and growing in time the payment of a **National-Dividend** would abolish poverty and make economic security a fact.

3
The Importance of Banking

The credit to finance a National-Dividend would be created by the United States Treasury from a **National Credit Account**. It would be backed by the credit of the people of the United States — which is America's Real-Wealth. The dividend would be financed out of the increased real credit of the Nation.

As consumers cash their Dividend-Checks and exchange them for goods, the cancelled checks would return to the banks, to be charged against the **National Credit Account**. The credit represented by the Dividend would thus return to its source where it would be cancelled as production is consumed.

This is the reason for issuing the Dividend in the form of a check instead of currency. The amount of money represented by the Dividend would be used to finance consumption, and having served this purpose, the Dividend-Checks would return to their source (**The National Credit Account**), providing a safeguard against inflation.

The banks, as agents of the Treasury, would accept and cash the Dividend-Checks, handling these transactions exactly as they do now. Our present banking system has all the facilities necessary to carry out this function. The banks and their trained personnel are an essential factor in the practical administration of Social Credit in this way,

The banks must continue to operate in every field of their public service, except for their power to create and destroy money at will, and for their services rendered they would be recompensed by service charges. No disruption of the banking system need attend such a Dividend.

This great association, the U.S.A., Inc., must continue to operate on a large scale or cease to exists. We have the materials, the equipment, the power, and the skill, to produce at least three times as much Wealth as we do now. Only the lack of money prevents us from doing so; a shortage of buying-power denies us the prosperity and the dividends that our resources justify. How long will the shareholders tolerate this shortage, when necessity demands that we declare dividends and achieve a prosperity never before experienced?

We must understand of course that the payment of salaries and wages would continue as at present, based on the worker's contribution to society. The economic and social usefulness of each worker must always govern earning-power. But we definitely know from practical experience of the present and the past that the aggregate of salaries and wages, no matter how high they maybe raised, can never purchase the total of the goods that industry has the capacity to produce.

Raising wages and limiting hours of work cannot solve this problem that results in depressions. Buying-power must be increased from some source that does not increase costs and thus raise prices. A **National-Dividend** would break this vicious circle. The Dividend is the logical answer to the problem of a living wage.

Our minds have been so trained to accept scarcity that it is difficult at first to realize the physical and spiritual benefits resulting from equating buying-power with the price of production in this country. Maybe it sounds too technical if we speak of it in this way. But the Dividend would not only stimulate business with a new demand for goods; the creation of new and richer human values in the life of every citizen would be more valuable than the material benefits gained. A new understanding growing out of the mutual cooperation of man with man would enrich the experience of everyone on earth. The effects of this addition to the positive human values of our national life are beyond calculation.

Even so, the immediate need for a **National-Dividend** is economic: the need to provide for the millions now on relief by a direct draft upon our unused capacity to produce. The Dividend would deliver goods to consumers instead of destroying goods by the armaments of needless war. This sabotage of earthly goods would be stopped and surplus turned into useful supply.

4
The Dividend Is Not A Dole

Some people on hearing for the first time of the **National-Dividend,** fear that it may be some sort of "dole." The Dividend is not a dole. A dole, like our present relief program, robs Peter to pay Paul. A dole takes money by taxation from the already inadequate incomes of the employed to support the unemployed. The dole does not add a penny to the national income.

The Dividend, on the other hand, is a means of tapping a new reservoir of credit unused today, but immediately available and necessary to distribute the goods America can produce. The Dividend would add directly to the national income, and to every shopper and consumer of goods, would represent the right to share in the benefits of the modern civilization.

Some people might imagine that the Dividend would breed laziness, like some forms of welfare today. To begin with, the Dividend, would not be large enough to support any one in luxury. It would be increased only as the National Wealth increases.

But aren't there always some people, we may ask, who are lazy and would rather exist on a subsistence standard of living than exert themselves in order to have more? Perhaps there are, and such people are supported today by the rest of us. We maintain these drones out of our own personal income and this would become unnecessary.

From Debt To Prosperity

5

The Blessing of Leisure Time

The subject of the **National-Dividend** is a fascinating one from both the economic and human points of view. But despite its many advantages we shall conclude this subject with the fact that **with a National-Dividend we would abolish Poverty**. It would bring economic security to all consumers and put an end to the exploitation of human labor by the few.

To be released from all forced labor, and to engage only in voluntary work, whilst security and plenty are assured to all, has been the motive force behind every invention and discovery since the great industrial awakening began.

As machines replace men and eliminate human drudgery, the true dignity of labor is at last seen, and the curse of what we now call unemployment will become the blessing of leisure time. This leisure represents time for education and recreation in their fullest sense, the enjoyment of books, the arts, the outdoors, the opportunity for self-development and study.

Unemployment is a present fact, but when we create leisure, the present evil will become a true blessing indeed. Only through leisure do we find the opportunity to cultivate and multiply human values and the mind.

6
Economic Security For All

What are we trying to achieve? What are we aiming at? We are endeavouring to bring a New Civilization to birth. We are doing something which really extends far beyond the confines of a change in the system. We are endeavouring by chiefly financial means, to enable the community to step out of one type of civilization into another type, based on Economic Security that is absolute.

In considering the **Retail-Discount** and the **National-Dividend,** we have noted some of the many advantages contained in each. But we must understand that **both the National-Dividend and a Just-Price would be inseparably linked together in a constructive economic program overall.**

The importance of a coordinated functioning of the two cannot be overstated. Both must operate together. The **Just-Price** to be covered below equates purchasing-power with total retail prices, prevents inflation and stabilizes price levels. The **National-Dividend** supplies buying-power to those of us who have none at present. **The two would be conjoined in purpose, in operation, and in effect.**

The outworn financial formulas of the past can never find the way out by burying us under new and higher mountains of debt. The way out of our present enslavement to debt is not through more debt, **it is through the use of the Real-Credit that we have.**

The knowledge of what Social Credit is and how it will provide Economic Security for all is essential to every intelligent individual American today. The issuance of National-Credit directly to consumers, based on America's Real-Wealth, is our greatest prime necessity. How long must the **manufactured illusion of scarcity** stand between our physical needs and the Real-Wealth that is ours? The opportunity to grasp Prosperity is here at hand; we must take it now, or continue to struggle with Poverty.

The reform suggested is not put forward as an alternative to **Capitalism** but as an alternative to **Chaos.** So long as the present system provides the majority of people with a living of some sort, no alternative, however attractive, has much chance of being considered. But when it becomes obvious that the system is breaking down the only alternative that will succeed is the one that will reconcile the greatest number of interests with the minimum of disturbance. The Social Credit proposals will fulfill these conditions. They can make the poor rich without making the rich poor, and involve no change in administration, only a change in financial policy.

The breakdown of the present financial and social system is certain. We must decide to master the mighty economic and social machine that we have created, or let it master us. **And that impetus from a body of men who know what to do and how to do it** may make the difference between another retreat into the Dark Ages, or an emergence into a full light of a day of such splendor as we can only at present imagine.

We are just beginning to realize that **human values** are equally as important as **money-values**. But we can never truthfully say that *"we love our neighbor as ourselves"* until we have been freed to live together liberated from our slavery to money.

Wishing and waiting will not solve the problem — the necessity to act is now. Day-by-day we are being driven in the direction of the Social Credit proposals referred to in this book. In the Government's failing struggle to overcome the problems of unbearable taxation and of unpayable debt, and in the coming turn of events, **Social Credit provides the only known means for increasing buying-power while at the same time preventing inflation.**

When the **hypnotic spell of the illusion of money-scarcity** begins to lose its hold over awakening Americans, the servitude of man to money will at last be abolished and economic security for all will become a fact.

Why?

From Debt To Prosperity

There are people badly housed, people badly fed, insufficient wages. Entire countries are suffering from hunger.

Every Christian must make it his duty to fight and replace an economic system that mass-produces poor homeless, helpless, starving people.

7

God Or Mammon?

Frustrated before plenty:

Though the ills of society, economic and political, are obvious and menacing, their real causation must be discovered by accurate diagnosis before they can be remedied.

What is the purpose of the industrial (and economic) organization of society? Is it to provide employment — work — for all? Or is it to produce, and make available to everyone, material goods and services with the least *possible amount of work?*

The process of increasing the efficiency of productive human labor — and of gradually diminishing the amount of labor required by supplementing it with labor-saving machinery — has reached the stage at which society can now make available the material necessities of life for all with a steadily diminishing amount of human labor.

But this organization has failed to deliver for use more than a fraction of the wealth which it is equipped to produce, so that the public does not yet realize the enormous productive capacity of the industrial system, and it still believes that a sufficiency of wealth can only be produced by the whole population laboring as long and as hard as people had to work ages ago, before modern labor-saving machinery were invented.

Hence, machinery is blamed as a curse as it is being more and more held idle. People in general are just beginning to realize that the world, under the capitalist industrial and economic regime, has reached the age of possible plenty. They hear of millions of tons of wheat being destroyed; crops being deliberately reduced; wealth in a variety of forms being destroyed in war instead of being distributed for consumption; men willing to work are kept idle; machines and factories running part time in all countries; while millions of the world's population are destitute, because the system is failing to distribute the increasing wealth which it could produce if it were permitted to do so.

But while people rightly cry out for reform, they are mostly unaware of actually what is wrong, and hence clamor for futile and unlawful schemes of reform.

These schemes are **Communism** and **Socialism** — unlawful because they deny natural human rights; futile, because they wrongly diagnose, and would therefore fail to cure, the economic evils from which society is suffering.

If we are to find the right remedy, we must diagnose the disease aright. The natural purpose of all economic and industrial association is to provide material goods and services for use and consumption. To serve this end, two processes are needed: **production of products**, including transport, and **distribution of products** by exchange (trade, commerce).

Production and transportation is becoming ever more efficient. Therefore, the defect lies in the latter; **product distribution has broken down.**

The medium of distribution is money. The monetary system is not functioning as it should: i.e. is not delivering the goods.

The defective monetary system:

Money is a system of **tickets of exchange**, the value and validity of which are based on men's belief (credibility) in the wealth-producing capacity of the community using them. Its sole function is to ensure that all the wealth that the community is capable of producing be continuously produced and exchanged among consumers for its use.

It is the duty of the State to so control the issuing of money-tickets for the *production of wealth,* and the cancelling of them through the *consumption of wealth,* that the system effectively discharge these functions.

But all modern governments have neglected this duty by giving the money system to unfettered groups of private citizens, who ignore the essential purpose of the system and make it a subversive, anti-social monopoly of political and economic power in their hands.

The controllers of this financing or banking system issue the community's money-tickets (for wealth-production and distribution) as a debt to themselves (at interest), and cancel these money-tickets when repaid, for a percentage of the wealth produced, thus causing an ever-widening gap between the community's purchasing-power as consumers, and the total wealth which the community has produced for the consumers' use.

Hence the forced export of goods and the competitive struggle of nations for foreign markets. Hence the accumulation of international debt and economic conflict leading to war. Hence the progressive mortgaging of society's capital, industrial plants, and wealth producing sources to the monopoly of world banks.

The State has become a slave:

Another disastrous consequence is the enslavement of the State to a superstate plutocracy in which political power is usurped and wielded by the controllers of the very lifeblood of economics and industry, which is finance.

Hence the utter perversion of order of the industrial and economic organization, when the authority of this latter ought to be supreme. This authority derives rightly from God, not from the superior might of those who have usurped economic domination and are swayed by greed for power.

As a consequence of the financial impoverishment of the masses, and of mortgaging the community's capital and wealth-producing sources to the finance-controllers, the State has to take over and administered many of the economic organs of the State.

But they can accomplish this purpose only if the State makes the money system subserve industry by legally directing this money system to keep the products of the community's industry (as producers) distributed for use to the community (as consumers).

It is the duty of those commissioned to teach and to rule, *whether in Church or in State,* not only to formulate sound practical principles for the guidance of men in their social, political, and economic relations, but also to study the actual conditions prevailing in those relations, so as to be able rightly to apply the principles to the facts, for the elimination of abuses and the amelioration of conditions.

Society has been robbed of its credit:

The banking system alone, has and exercises de facto the power of creating and cancelling money.

The value, validity, and purchasing power of this money rests ultimately not on gold, but on the National-Credit, i.e., the community's potential rate of producing Real-Wealth compared with consumption.

Therefore, the community should not be forced to pay a perpetual money levy to private creators and issuers of money for its creation and issue. The community is forced to pay such a levy, and this in money which only the bankers can create.

This payment of interest by the community to the banking system for money newly created (and costless) is on a wholly different footing from interest charged on money already circulating by individuals who have earned and saved this money, and invested it in (or lent it to) industry.

Consequences:

The consequences of this failure of money to discharge its essential function are disastrous and cumulative:

a) Cut-throat competition to recover proportionately the greatest sum in prices in return for the least volume of goods sold;

b) A steady stream of bankruptcies (of the weaker and less aggressive producers) as an inevitable result of the mathematical impossibility of recovering for the banks more money than exists in the community;

c) The replacing of competition by monopolistic rings to raise prices;

d) The growing accumulation of an unsaleable surplus in each capitalist country;

e) The forced export of this surplus and consequent struggle for foreign markets, ending in international economic and military conflicts;

f) The development of the banking policy of financing capital equipment to provide consumers with money to purchase some of the otherwise unsaleable surplus of consumers' goods;

g) The gradual breakdown of this device, owing partly to substitution of machinery for human and wage-paid employment, and partly through the capital equipment becoming excessive and lying idle (through lack of consumer's incomes which would purchase its ultimate products).

The true remedy:

The governments want to remedy these situations through various palliatives, through public works, or direct aid to the most destitute. And the governments can get the money necessary for these remedies only by two ways:

a) Through taxes taken on the already insufficient incomes of the consumers;

b) Through loans from the banks of new money created by the banks, which must be repaid with the interest.

The failure of these remedies is obvious. They will leave the consumers with a bigger debt and less purchasing power. To solve the problem, governments must:

a) Take back their prerogative and exercise the control over the volume of money required for the population themselves;

b) Base the money on the productive capacity of the country;

c) Issue new money no longer as an interest-bearing debt to the bankers, but debt-free;

d) Provide a **National-Dividend** to each citizen.

At the same time, in order to automatically prevent any inflation or deflation of prices, and to maintain a constant balance between prices and purchasing-power, prices must be subjected to a **National-Discount,** set in accordance with the statistics of production and consumption. This discount will be calculated to fill the gap between prices and collective purchasing-power.

From Debt To Prosperity

8
Facing The Facts Of Today

In recent years we have been suffering from a world-wide Depression. We experience want in the midst of plenty, surrounded by an abundance of the things we need.

But this sorry situation becomes even more vivid when we compare **Producing America** with **Consuming America.**

When we compare America the Manufacturer with America the Shopper we find that the manufacturer can produce more than the shopper can buy. In this situation the machinery of business is stalled.

Business recovery means economic recovery.

Economics is a matter of everyday business experience for it is the housekeeping business of society. Everyone in business is familiar with economics by practical experience.

We needn't fear economics as something that is difficult to understand for we can talk about it in simple everyday words. Instead of struggling to grasp a mass of abstract ideas it is much better to think of economics simply as everybody's everyday business.

If we are to talk about business we must begin by defining it so that we may know just what business is. Business is the process of satisfying our needs and desires with goods in exchange for money, which is called business or trade.

Business must be conducted because its transactions satisfy our desires for goods. We have a constant need for goods and an abundant means for producing them. To understand the meaning of economic recovery requires first that we know what the purpose of the economic system is.

Purpose of the Economic System:
Picture a vast plate glass shopwindow, reaching all the way across the continent from New York to San Francisco.

Inside that window are all the goods that America makes. Outside of it are millions of us, would-be shoppers, with our noses flattened against the window just as we used to do when we were children.

Let's go into the shop and see what we find there.

The first thing that impresses us is the amazing variety of goods that are for sale in the shop. There are almost a million items offered for sale — everything that we need in order to live in comfort and convenience and satisfaction.

Suppose we ask the shopkeeper how he can maintain this supply of goods? He will show us warehouses bulging with goods. Beyond the warehouses is a chain of factories and beyond the factories are farms and mines, and beyond those, laboratories and schools, and back of all these things is the American people themselves with their ambitions, their enthusiasms, their inventiveness and their history. With these resources the shopkeeper can guarantee to provide us with a supply of goods beyond the limits of the imagination.

That supply of goods and services is America's Real-Wealth. The ability to produce and deliver these goods and services is the only true limit of our Real-Credit. Recent surveys show that our present productive capacity can supply goods and services to every family in the nation at the rate of at least $250,000 a year. So there is no question about the abundance of our tangible Real-Wealth.

As we look around in this workshop of wealth, we remark how few people are working in it. Everywhere we look we see labor-saving machinery that has been designed and installed purposely to eliminate human drudgery. Thanks to Science, the curse of Adam has been lifted from the backs of men and transferred to the backs of Nature's forces by means of power: steam, fuel, and electrical energy. Our control over these forces can keep the shopwindow filled with goods, yet we have just begun to use our mechanical servants efficiently. The sight of all the goods they can produce in the store of plenty should make us feel very wealthy.

Now let's join the millions of shoppers outside the window. What a change we find here! Instead of the orderly scientific cooperation of the productive system and all the abundance of goods created by it, when we get outside we find a struggling crowd of anxious and worried people.

Everyone is elbowing everyone else and most of us seem to be getting the worst of it.

All of us are shoppers and consumers of goods. We need food, clothing, and shelter in order to live. We have, besides, many other desires we would like to satisfy.

Why have we built up this vast store of wealth and all the activities necessary to maintain its supply?

As shoppers and consumers of goods, if we ask ourselves this question the answer is obvious. **We produce goods in order that we may consume them. The purpose of production is consumption.** All of us know from experience that there are many goods and services that we must obtain from others who are better able to supply them than we are. Some systematic process for the production and distribution of these goods is necessary if we are to work together in an orderly and intelligent fashion. So modern business developed and its enormous capacity to produce goods and render services is now highly specialized.

Briefly, we may define the purpose of **the economic system** by saying that **it exists to deliver goods and services as, when, and where they are required for consumption and use.**

With this purpose clearly in mind and remembering that we are to contrast America the Manufacturer with America the Shopper, let us look at our economic system of today.

The general facts of **our present difficulties** are painfully familiar to all of us by personal experience.

They may be classified in four main groups: **Poverty, Debt, Taxation, and Depression**. It is hard to say which of these is the heaviest curse on our 21st Century civilization. But it is significant that all four are found together in this, the greatest age of science and power over nature, man has ever known.

The Paradox of Plenty:

Thanks to science we have at last achieved the long desired age of plenty. Inventions and technological advances have, almost unbelievably, increased our capacity to produce Real-Wealth in the United States, yet we cannot distribute the consumable goods that we even now produce. And at least half of this **immense productive capacity** lies idle.

Producers wish to sell. But distributors, dare not buy because they cannot sell to consumers. Shoppers are eager to buy. Many are homeless, hungry, and cold. But they cannot eat or clothe themselves, or find shelter, for they have no money to purchase what the producer wishes to sell to them.

This is the famous Paradox, "poverty in the midst of plenty", a humiliating state of misery in the richest nation on earth. All this suffering is due to a glut of goods, to the very surplus of wealth itself.

Ninety percent of the population of the United States does not get enough to live on in decent security. More than thirty million people are living at a mere subsistence level, with barely enough food to keep them alive, a roof over their heads, and clothing to cover their bodies.

Taxation and Debt; and Increases To Come:

Meanwhile business stagnates for lack of sales, and we struggle under increasing taxation and debt.

Increasing governmental expenditures for recovery and relief must be paid principally out of more and higher taxes. As taxpayers we are all headed for the day of drawing our belts still tighter over already empty stomachs. For the skyrocket of climbing taxation is on the way up, and the zenith of its course, will bring an explosion of national bankruptcies. Must we patiently sit by waiting for this to happen?

Growing welfare and relief funds add to the burden of those who are employed. And already these funds are proving insufficient to provide a decent share of food, clothing, and shelter for the unemployed and their families.

The total number of persons now unemployed, in the United States, is estimated in the millions. Most of these people are willing and eager to work, but we cannot find jobs for them. Yet somehow they must live. So to supply them with food, clothing, and shelter, we supply them out of public funds, in the name of unemployment relief. Where do these funds come from? The Government derives them mainly from taxes, so that in effect **all of the taxpayers are employing the unemployed.**

Even though the funds immediately necessary for relief are raised through bond issues, taken up mostly by banks, the bonds themselves must eventually be repaid out of taxation. We are merely piling future debt upon present debt, mortgaging the future to pay for the confusion of today.

The efforts of the government to distribute additional purchasing power through loans, civil and public works programs, relief measures and the requirements of Congress have increased employment and stimulated some producers, but the buying-power reaching the hands of the nation's shoppers has been insufficient to absorb the total of this production. Admittedly, Congress has reduced unemployment, but many of the people thus employed are working part time, on hours and wages so short that they do not actually receive half of the minimum wage requirements. The steady march of technological progress cannot be halted simply by limiting hours of work and over-burdening the payrolls of business.

Approximately one out of every seven of our population is dependent on welfare and relief funds.

It has been estimated that the sum spent on government welfare equals the stupendous figure of $12,000 dollars per minute. **This money is being borrowed**, mainly from the banking system through government bond issues. At the same time statisticians estimate that more than 85% of the business assets in the United States are mortgaged to the banking system.

Yet the attitude prevails that repayment of our National Debt is a minor thing to be concerned about at the moment and we can go right on borrowing and **enjoy spending ourselves rich.** This is planned as the practical way *out of our present poverty!*

How can more debt be the way out of our present indebtedness? We might as well try to stop the weather from getting cold by taking off more clothes.

The Stupidity of Sabotage:

We also have the surprising spectacle of an organized and government-sanctioned plan of sabotage — the deliberate destruction of agricultural wealth by restricting production to the level of current consumption. How can wealth be made available to needy consumers by withholding it? Obviously the destruction of wealth also destroys corresponding human satisfactions.

Writing in a national magazine of man's agelong dream of plenty for all, and his present inability to manage his own affairs, an Editor says:

"In the very act of seizing the reality of unlimited plenty man is frustrated, not by anything that happens untowardly to the dream itself, *but because the dream comes true.* Plenty overwhelms him. He cannot manage it. And when he tries to say why, what he says does not make sense. Because people can produce more than they can consume, they cannot consume as much as they need and want."

Does that make sense? Yet he must behave as if it does, unable to think what else to do. Never was worse confusion. The wonderful economic mechanism we had been boasting about has gone absurdly wrong.

Plain Facts:

Certainly our rich natural resources, our fields and mines and factories, with all their productive ability, exist today as they did in 1929. And with still more certainty we know that the needs and desires of our millions of people for food, clothing, and shelter, to say nothing of such things as radios, TVs, warm blankets, and automobiles, are as great, if not greater, than they ever were in times past.

Yet we are told now that we are in debt. The "financial experts" report that in terms of money more than two thirds of our wealth has vanished into thin air.

Now, if two thirds of our country had been destroyed by earthquake, fire, or flood we could understand how two thirds of our wealth might have been destroyed. But there has been no such catastrophe. Nature has been kind to us. America is here as beautiful and plentiful as ever, with her rich crops and her factories filled with machinery.

What has happened to this wealth that has made it lose its value? Nothing at all. **The wealth itself still exists, but its value in terms of money has been practically destroyed.** We have made the fatal mistake of confusing our WEALTH figures with MONEY, and we have thusly deprived ourselves of the wealth we need.

Outside the shopwindow of plenty we stand looking in and wishing for more money, for more buying-power. Discouraged and bewildered, we yearn for the wealth of goods in the window when it is denied us simply by limitations of our own creating; **limitation of our Money System.** What a tragic absurdity; it is doubly stupid because it can be changed whenever we decide to change it.

Bewildered Business:

Let's try to put the problem simply and precisely. Working from the known facts will perhaps give us a clue to the answer. Industrial engineers testify that we are able to produce in abundance all we require to satisfy our needs. Then why don't we do so? **Because we have already produced more than we can sell.**

Our clue must lie somewhere in this so-called **"over-production."**

Why can't we sell these "surplus goods?" Because there is not enough buying-power in the country to equal the prices of the goods that we have produced. "The trouble is not lack of desire, **but lack of purchasing-power."**

This shortage of buying-power in the hands of would-be shoppers is deliberately built into our money system itself. Yet money has been devised by man as a means for carrying on business.

Is it possible, that as business operates today, there must always exist this unsalable surplus that we absurdly name **"over-production?"**

It is ridiculous to talk of over-production so long as consumers need goods and wish to buy them. Over-production is a stupid falsity so long as there is **unsatisfied demand**.

Under-Consumption; and Why:

Now we are getting close to the heart of the problem. Our difficulty is not concerned with **over-production** but with **under-consumption** instead. To be able to buy goods consumers must have buying-power. But there is a shortage of this necessary buying-power. **Under-consumption** exists because we have not sufficient **purchasing-power** to buy the total of the goods we produce.

There is ample provision for **financing production** but little and faulty provision for **financing consumption.** Producers **can produce** but consumers **cannot consume.**

Why do consumers lack buying-power? The answer is to be found in the financial system itself. This constant lack of buying-power exists because **lack is inherent in the money system itself.** It has two fundamental defects, so serious that the system has broken down. These defects are the root cause of *depression, poverty, taxation,* and *debt,* because they give birth to a chronic shortage of buying-power. **This shortage has been with us both in good times and bad, in times of "depression" and times of "prosperity."**

The Failure of Finance:

There must be no quibbling about the breakdown in the functioning of the money system. It is a fact. This is a serious charge, but there is ample evidence that it is well founded. The evidence is apparent not only in the records of what has happened; it is vividly demonstrated in our every-day experience.

The failure of the money system is felt by everyone, even little children, though they do not understand why they suffer. For the facts of modern money are quietly hushed in the newspapers, and the attention of the public distracted from the cause of its privations.

We may well remember the 1929 crash and its sudden destruction of financial values, when our national income shrank from 81 billion in 1929 to 48 billion in 1932. Or we may recall the **"bank holiday"** (what a happy name for it!)

of March 1933 with its freezing of deposits, and the subsequent withdrawal from circulation of all the gold upon which our money is supposed to be based; the international failure of the gold standard; the necessity of the government's present deposit insurance guarantee plan, designed purely to stimulate confidence in the banking system; the wholesale default of bonds and mortgages; the failures of insurance companies and investment houses; and a long list of personal failures resulting in new **all-time highs for suicide.**

We know personally the pressure of the present scarcity of money and credit both for business and consumers, and the prevailing misery of our mortgaged and debt-ridden population.

Awakened by suffering, public interest has at last begun to focus upon this **shortage of buying-power.** The failure of the money system to accomplish the smooth flow of goods from producer to consumer can no longer be concealed. Let us face the facts.

What has caused the Fall of our financial structure?

With the coming of Power, Money has failed man. So long as production remained difficult, and goods were relatively scarce, our antiquated money system could operate well enough to enable business to continue. **New markets were constantly being opened up to absorb the surplus of our production.** But today, when we are able, through the use of power machinery, to produce on the greatest scale in history, **the money system has not been adjusted to meet these new conditions.** Science and invention have outgrown our old ideas about money.

To understand why this has happened, and to see clearly the basic cause of our chronic shortage of buying power, we must first know how the money system works in practical operation. Since its operation has resulted in failure we must discover the facts behind this failure. We have seen that **the lack of buying-power is responsible for under-consumption.**

Now, let's determine what causes this chronic shortage of money.

9

Three Important Words

In every discussion about the money system we find three words frequently recurring. These three words are put to a great deal of abuse. And if we are to understand clearly why the operation of the money system produces a chronic and increasing **shortage of purchasing-power,** we must first have a definite understanding of these three words. They are all vitally related to each other. But their meaning has become confused.

The Meaning of WEALTH:

The first of these words is Wealth. Wealth has been defined by Webster as *"Large possessions, a comparative abundance of things desired, especially of worldly estate."*

From this definition it is apparent that wealth consists largely of goods. *"All things possess the attribute of wealth if they can be used directly or indirectly for the satisfaction of human desire."* The term wealth is thus a word used to express **the total of goods which can satisfy human desire, as well as the means of producing such goods.**

In considering our Wealth as a nation we must include as a very important part **the great Cultural Heritage that has been handed down to us by our forefathers.** The rich natural resources, the farms and factories which make America wealthy, would be of little use and could never have evolved were it not for the **organized scientific knowledge bequeathed to us by our ancestors.** This part of our wealth is an asset belonging to the entire nation.

The modern economic production system is not a system of individual production and exchange of production between individuals. It is more and more the synthetic assembly, in a central pool, of wealth consisting of goods and services which are primarily due to the use of power, to modern scientific processes, and all sorts of organizations. **The real wealth of any person, or of any nation, may be measured by his or its ability to deliver wanted services and goods.**

It is not always easy to measure wealth, for the value of any one article of Wealth depends directly upon the desire that people have for that article. But since we must all deal in wealth to satisfy our desires, it is essential to have some means of measuring its value in relation to our desires for the goods which compose wealth.

The necessity for dealing with wealth leads directly to the second of the words we must define in order to understand the money system. **This word is Credit.**

CREDIT; Real and Financial:

"Credit is the vital air of modern commerce." (Daniel Webster).

The word Credit comes from the Latin "credere" meaning "to believe."

"Credit...is something founded on belief." All of us use the word "credit", and when we say a man's credit is good we mean simply that **we have confidence in his ability to make good on his promise to pay.** In other words credit rests upon the ability to pay or to "deliver the goods" as promised.

But it is not generally realized that **there are two different and distinct kinds of credit,** known respectively as Real-

Credit and Financial-Credit.

Real-Credit may be defined as **the rate at which goods and services can be delivered, as, when, and where required.**

Financial-Credit may similarly be defined as **the rate at which money can be delivered**.

The inclusion in both definitions of the word "rate" is of course important.

Thus **Real-Credit** depends upon the ability to deliver goods and services. **Financial-Credit** depends upon the ability to deliver money as required. This distinction is very important and we must have it clearly in mind as we consider the monetary system. Let us note it well, for we shall refer to it later.

What is MONEY:

The third word we must understand clearly is Money. Money is the "Title to Life" in modern society. But there is probably no other word in our language about which there is so much muddled thinking and confusion. It is no exaggeration to say that most of the wreckage in our stalled economic machinery is due to a misunderstanding of the true nature and function of Money. Therefore it is vital to understand Money itself, even though this may require some revision of our former notions.

Money has been defined as a "medium of exchange" or a "means of expressing an effective demand for goods." In these days of economic hysteria this simple definition will remove much of the confusion that shrouds money in mystery.

We read and hear a great deal about "sound money." What is this "sound money" the experts talk about? Certainly it is sensible to say that a "sound money system" is a system that works — a system that makes effective the existing demand for goods.

Money and Gold:

The origin of the use of money was lost in the beginning of history. Originally men satisfied their desires by barter, by exchanging goods for goods. As time went on however it was found more convenient to effect exchanges by means of some sort of **objects of value** such as cattle, hides, or gold. Later these gave way to metal discs and eventually coins, serving the purpose of accepted **measurements of value** issued by governments as **currency; government money.** Because gold was both scarce and easy to measure, it was used for coins and gradually became accepted as the basis of the value of money. Gold, which is simply one commodity, thus grew to be considered the foundation of the early monetary system.

When merchants, in the later Middle Ages, felt the need of some safe place in which to store their money ... the only people inspiring them with sufficient confidence were the goldsmiths, and the practice arose of depositing money with them. At first when a merchant had payments to make he would withdraw his money (his gold) to enable him to do so. Later on he merely gave an order to the goldsmith to pay over the necessary sum with warehouse receipts.

But as the trading of wealth increased, paper money or **"notes"** gradually supplanted the handling of gold. **Metallic money gave way to paper notes about 1700 A.D.** and the goldsmiths went into the banking business. From this we have evolved a still more convenient system: our banks, by extending credits, enable their depositors to issue bank-money, by signing checks, which circulates so acceptably that it is now used for most of our transactions. Today this bank-money amounts to **more than eleven times** the currency-money issued by the Government.

One important point here deserves our consideration. Before checks came into use gold was the chief measure of value upon which money was issued. **Now that we use checks,** and gold is out of circulation (most of the countries of the world having "gone off the Gold Standard" and our dollar having been **devalued or "clipped"**), the money system has become more and more a **bookkeeping method** to record values exchanged, and no longer dependent upon gold.

Some people still maintain that the price of gold is the only standard of value, but both history and present experience challenge this belief. On this point even the Supreme Court has been called into controversy! But, for two good reasons, we need not waste time on this conflict.

In the first place, we are concerned chiefly with the practical workings of the money system now that gold is out of circulation. And secondly, we have defined money simply as a medium of exchange, and we are observing the actual operation of this medium in business.

From Debt To Prosperity

10
The Nature Of Money

We know then that goods are conveyed from Producer to Consumer by means of money. Money is thus the **connecting link** between production and consumption. It acts as a bridge between the **desire for goods** on the part of the consumer and the **supply of goods** on the part of the producer. We might say that money is the **equalizing medium** between desire and goods, enabling the one to be satisfied in terms of the other. It functions as an invisible force of which, like electricity running a motor, we see only its effects transforming desire, which is mental, into physical goods which represent the satisfaction of that desire.

From this it should be plain that **money is something numerical,** not a material substance. **Money is not wealth itself, but a symbol of wealth,** and a means of measuring its value. Money gives us a method for applying **number-values** to goods.

If we stick to personal experience, we cannot fail to realize that **money is but a ticke**t, a ticket authorizing us to shop in the nation's Storehouse of Wealth. Money permits us to **claim** a portion of the wealth in the store. A **money-ticke**t is exactly like a **railroad-ticket** except that a railroad-ticket is only good for transportation while a money-ticket is good for anything in the store up to its stated value in prices.

We thus arrive at a true conception of the nature of money; money is simply **a social mechanism** designed to facilitate orderly **production and distribution.** The money system is to all intents and purposes merely a **system of**

tickets entitling the holder to goods and services of his choice. Above all, **money, as such, is not a commodity;** it has no intrinsic value apart from the function it performs, and to regard money as a commodity is proof of a radical misunderstanding of that function.

Money is not a commodity of substance, having size, shape, and weight, like wheat or steel. Thinking about money as a commodity, such as gold, instead of as **a measure of value,** causes much of our confusion today. **Commodities fluctuate in value according to supply and demand,** so no one commodity by itself is suitable as an absolute measurement of value for other commodities.

Gold is the worst commodity of all to choose as a money substitute.

Money is the keystone which holds our economic structure together. The reason why money is so important that people quarrel about it, is that these money-tickets are indispensable to our shopping. Money-tickets are as necessary to our shopping as shopping is to our lives. In civilized society our lives depend upon money and the money system. For without money that works, that is "sound," we cannot grasp any of the wealth that fills the shops of America.

But to deserve the name "sound," money must possess **two important qualifications**. For one thing, it must have **acceptability**, which means simply that everyone who uses it has confidence that it can be exchanged for wanted goods or services. And secondly, since it is the medium of exchange, money should **accurately express the current demand for available goods.**

In short, any sort of a sound money system must reflect the true facts of production. It must provide enough of the means of exchange to keep goods moving from producers to the shoppers who consume the goods.

Two Kinds of Money:

As we have already seen, **there are mainly two kinds of money in use today.** First is **currency**, or tangible government money which circulates as coins; pennies, nickels, dimes, quarters, and dollar bills. Second is **credit-money**, or bank deposits circulating as **checks**.

Currency is only the pin-money of business. Checks are used in practically all large transactions, where coins or bills are not convenient. In fact, **more than 90% of our business is done with checks** (credit-money).

Currency is issued by the government as coins or printed bills, but many people do not know how credit-money comes into existence. We use checks because they are safe and handy, they can be written for transforming wealth of an exact amount, to specific individuals, and so long as they are acceptable we think no more about it.

The Birth and Death of Credit-Money:

Suppose we look into the source of this credit-money with which we do at least 90% of our buying and selling. Where is it born? We know that **a check is an order against a bank balance.** The bank balance consists of deposits credited to an account. These deposits themselves may be in the form of checks drawn upon other accounts. No currency actually changes hands in paying for goods or services with this kind of money. Complicated transactions involving immense sums of money are handled purely by means of the **bookkeeping** carried on by the banks, entering credits and debits on their books. In their bookkeeping the banks *credit* (*add to*) and *debit* (*deduct from*) the accounts of their customers.

It is clear from this that whatever money was intended to accomplish by means of currency, it is a different story today now that we write checks. **The check-system is simply a series of bookkeeping entries**, and our monetary system functions mainly as the circulation of these checks.

We do almost all of our business by means of bits of paper, or computer key strokes, which are evidences of Financial-Credit. **And this credit itself is created or destroyed in the bookkeeping processes of the banks.** The checks system is in itself a great advance upon the use of tickets in many ways. But its invention has resulted in the banks, not coining money, as that is quite unnecessary, **but creating money with computer key strokes without even issuing printed notes.**

The method by which the banker makes money is ingenious and consists largely of **bookkeeping.** This kind of money is born in a bank and dies in a bank. And the bank is responsible both for its birth and its death. The banker creates the means of payment out of nothing at all.

The fact that banks create and destroy money by the bookkeeping process of **issuing or cancelling credits** is illustrated by any ordinary bank loan. Suppose we go to the bank to borrow $1,000. The banker passes judgment on our credit rating, **accepts our promissory note as a gift,** and grants the loan, crediting our account exactly as though we had deposited this sum in cash. We are now **"in debt"** to the banker. We owe him the $1,000 we have borrowed, **plus the interest he charges us for its use.** We can then write checks against our **new account,** and these checks are acceptable as money.

Now, the banks are permitted to lend up to ten times their actual cash reserve, and in so doing **the banker "creates" — in the case of our loan — $10,000** (*less interest*) **in new money.**

But when the time comes to repay this sum the credit he has extended to us is destroyed. We can no longer write checks against it. Indeed, we must pay the banker promptly or forfeit whatever security has been placed with him as collateral. **If we cannot pay, our security then passes into his hands. In other words, every bank loan creates a deposit and every repayment of a bank loan destroys the deposit.**

Loans are made and deposits created by crediting the borrower's account in the banker's book. And the money thus created is destroyed in the same way, by debiting the borrower's account. What has it cost the bank to lend us $1,000? **Nothing but the expense incurred in its bookkeeping.**

As a result of the bookkeeping process of the banks, **new money is constantly being created and destroyed.** And this money to be created "out of nothing," said by the Encyclopedia Britannica, is being manufactured out of little more than pen, paper, confidence, and some ink.

This bookkeeping process — the banking method governing the birth and death of money — is clearly described by Reginald McKenna, Chairman of the Midland Bank of London and former Chancellor of the Exchequer:

"The amount of money in existence varies only with the action of the banks. **Every bank loan creates a deposit...** There is only one method by which we can add to or diminish the aggregate amount of our money... The amount of money in existence varies only with the action of the banks in increasing or diminishing deposits. We know how this is effected. **Every bank loan and every bank purchase of securities creates a deposit, and every repayment of a bank loan and every bank sale destroys one."** (Speech at General Meeting, *Midland Bank, Ltd.,* Jan. 25, 1924).

When we think of our own hard-earned personal bank accounts we perhaps imagine that our deposits are used by the banks to create new credit-money. But the banks do not, as many people believe, lend such deposits. By virtue of their privilege of lending up to ten times their cash reserves, **banks create Financial-Credit** which in their bookkeeping becomes a DEBT against the borrower.

The essential and distinctive feature of a 'bank' and a 'banker' is to create and issue credit payable on demand. This credit is intended to be put into circulation and serve all the purposes of money. A bank is not an office for borrowing and lending money, **it is a 'manufactory' of credit.** A deposit and an issue are the same thing. A banker's profit consists exclusively in the profits he can make by creating and issuing credit in excess of the specie (currency) he holds in reserve. A bank only begins to make profits when it creates and issues credit in exchange for debts payable at a future time.

It is not unnatural to think of the deposits of a bank as being created by the public through the deposit of cash representing either savings or amounts which are not for the time being required to meet expenditure, **but the bulk of the deposits arises out of the action of the banks**

themselves, for by granting loans, allowing money to be drawn on an overdraft, or by purchasing securities a bank creates a credit in its books which is the equivalent of a deposit.

Although, we are stressing the function of the banking system as a manufacturer of money, it is far from our object to impress the reader with any suspicion that such manufacture is criminal. Our object is to impress the reader with the importance of the fact that it is a private body, not responsible to the nation, which actually manufactures and controls the manufacture of money, and by so doing controls the nation's means of life.

Our Economic Blood:

Money circulates. This is a fact familiar to every one. In the economic system money may well be compared to the blood of the human body. Money in business is equally as vital as the blood in our bodies. It circulates, carrying life and vitality in its flow. Money is the medium of exchange. Business cannot survive without exchange. Exchange implies activity, and this activity is the flow of money, its circulation. The flow cannot cease, **for money satisfies desire only when it is exchanged for goods and services; it has no inherent value in itself.** Money itself cannot be worn or eaten but it can buy clothing to wear and food to eat. When money ceases to flow, its power to satisfy needs and desire dies, exactly as we die when our blood stops circulating. **Only so long as money circulates is business alive and healthy.**

We know the time blood takes to circulate through the human body. We measure its circulation by our pulse rate. And in just the same way, it takes time for money to circulate through business. Time and flow taken together give us a **rate of flow**, and this rate of flow is the way we measure the speed of the circulation of money.

But the likeness between money and blood is still closer. For both of them circulate. That is, the course of their flow is circular. Money tends to flow in a circle through business. Its circulation begins in a bank, since it is in the bank that most of our money is born. The banker, for example, makes a loan to a producer. The producer pays his workmen, executives and shareholders, who presently appear as shoppers, consumers of goods in the retail market. The retailer then pays the wholesaler, who in turn pays the producer, who at length repays his loan to the bank. Whereupon that amount of credit is destroyed until the bank makes a new loan, when it creates more new credit Then the circle is repeated. And business is dependent for its existence on this life-blood circulating in its economic body.

Business Versus DEBT:

Now our study of money grows exciting, for here we come face to face with Debt. We know debt well, for it is always at our door. And it poses as our friend Credit, a wolf in sheep's clothing. More than that, Debt plagues us always, since every bank loan, in creating a deposit, at once puts the borrower into debt. Banks, it is true, create "credit," which they are said to extend to borrowers. **But, the bank's "credit" becomes the borrower's "debt."** Strictly speaking, therefore, most of our business is done on the basis of debt, because the money thus created is issued as loans which must be repaid with interest.

The Deluge of Debt:

The old Biblical tale of Noah and the Flood has its modern parallel. We are told that in Noah's day the world was submerged under great waters. But our modern flood is even greater than Noah's and is just as real. For in our day we are steadily sinking under a deluge of debt. We are not thinking of War Debts, or of International Debts, or of any relatives of these which may be in the limelight at any given moment, but of the system itself by which **all money is debt payable to the banking system.**

Struggle against this as we may, so long as money comes into being as a debt payable to the banking system we are its slaves. As Colbourne says, Even our vocabulary is perverted. When a bank is said to extend you "credit" it is doing nothing of the kind; it is extending you "debt."

It may be a disturbing thought to realize that the bulk of our money is debt-money, created by the banking system on the basis of the country's resources and its ability to deliver wanted goods. But however disturbing it may be, it is nevertheless true. **Our money is circulating evidence of debt to the banking system.** This is the solid fact which we must grasp: **The bulk of our money is Debt-Money payable to the non-federal Federal Reserve Bank.**

Unpayable Debt:

Is it any wonder that we sink in a flood of debt when every article of wealth we buy must be paid for with money which itself is debt? Debt surrounds us from birth to the grave. We cannot be rid of its grip because of the ingenious financially invented device called INTEREST.

The deluge of our present debt can never be drained away because **interest requires that the debtor repay more**

than has been loaned him. The process by which Debt-Money is created is cumulative — it grows. The debt cannot be liquidated because it grows faster than business can repay it. Debt can never be repaid, now or at any other time.

Thomas A. Edison is authority for the statement, *"In all our great bond issues the interest is always greater than the principal."* The total of principal and interest, which is more than the original loan, can be met only by the creation of more fresh debt to cover the interest. Thus debt breeds more debt, and the more we struggle the deeper we sink.

And our situation, bad as it appears now, is growing worse. For example, when we try to use this borrowed money to draw wealth from the shops of the nation **it becomes impossible, at the same time, to use the money to both draw wealth from the shops, and repay the debt**. If we borrow $5.00 to buy a pair of shoes, we have to choose between buying the pair of shoes and repaying the debt. If we choose to buy the shoes, we still owe the debt of $5.00. We can either have the shoes or pay the debt but we can't do both at once.

But this is not the whole story. Business depends upon the debt-money of the banking system. Every dollar loaned to business must be recovered in prices. Now, money is never borrowed except to be spent; but, as it must subsequently be repaid, the borrowers have to spend it in producing, or inducing the production of, something that can be sold; which means that **the harder the community works and the more it produces, the deeper it goes into debt to the banks.** So debt increases at the expense of our ability to buy goods.

It must, I think, be quite obvious to anybody that, if the world as a whole is consistently getting further and further into debt, it is not, as the ordinary business man would say, "paying its way" — The public is paying all that it can, and buying what it can. Its failure to pay more is therefore forcing the destruction of much production and is at the same time piling up more debt.

How fast does debt grow? "In the 17th century" (*that is to say, in the century in which the Bank of England was founded*) "the world debt" *(and we have plenty of accurate figures with regard to these matters)* "increased 47%. The Bank of England was founded at the end of the 17th century."

By the end of the 18th century the world debt had increased by 466 per cent, and by the end of the 19th century the world debt, public and private, had increased by 12,000%; and, according to some very exact calculations which have been carried out by a quite irreproachable professor of industrial engineering of Columbia University, Professor Rautenstrauch, taking the year 1800 as the origin and taking one hundred years as the unit, **the world debt is now increasing as the fourth power of time**; that is to say, increasing as time goes on, not as the square of time and not as the cube of time, but as the fourth power of time; and that is in spite of the numerous repudiations of debt, the writing down of debts, which takes place with every bankruptcy, and other methods to write off debts and start again.

The Key to Deliverance from Debt:

But we must not miss the one vital point which gives the key to this dilemma. The Debt-Money created and destroyed by banks is called "Financial-Credit," and in this term, the word "financial" deserves our attention.

The deluge of debt is purely financial debt since it is based upon what the banks call the "credit" that they create.

Now, we have already seen that there are two kinds of credit: Financial-Credit and Real-Credit, and herein lies our key. It was to make this point clear that we defined both Financial-Credit and Real-Credit before we began to examine the money system.

Later on we shall have occasion again to return to our definition of Real-Credit.

Our Findings Thus Far:

At this point we may well pause for a moment to sum up what we have found in the money system, and see what conclusions are possible. We can list our findings as follows:

1. Money is *not* wealth; money and wealth are two separate and distinct things.

2. Our modern money system has outgrown its former metallic coins and has become a system of bookkeeping.

3. More than 90% of our money is created and destroyed in the bookkeeping process of the private banking system. (*Practically all purchasing power comes into existence in the form of bank credits. Bank credits are created by the banks out of nothing.*)

4. Money comes into being as a debt which is loaned to us at interest by the private banking system. The economic blood circulating in the veins of business is the blood-money of debt.

The first conclusion that stands out from all of this is that **a money system built on debt and interest can function only to create more debt**. And this is precisely what has happened. The facts of experience confirm our findings.

The second conclusion, which is perhaps not quite so easy to see, is that under this system a shortage of money is inevitable, making it increasingly difficult to buy and exchange goods. There are two fundamental reasons for this and we shall begin with the simpler of the two.

From Debt To Prosperity

11
The Illusion Of Scarcity

We have already touched on the old idea that gold is the basis of money. It is true that gold, itself only one commodity among many, was used as money for centuries before the present "Age of Power" was ever dreamed of. But it is indeed strange to find financiers today still believing that this one commodity is the only basis of money in our complex twentieth century world of business. *"Money is gold, and nothing else,"* said J. P. Morgan.

Despite the absurdity of this statement many people have accepted it, and its acceptance has serious consequences.

Gold is a commodity whose supply is strictly limited; indeed, it is distinguished chiefly by its scarcity. Compared with the needs of industry and business gold is too scarce to be practical as money. And if the value of money is based on gold alone, it is an easy step from thinking of the commodity, gold, to thinking of money itself as a commodity. And the scarcity of gold can easily persuade many of us to accept, quite naturally, a corresponding scarcity of money.

If all the world's gold were sunk tomorrow in the middle of the Atlantic we could still write checks. How long will people tolerate this illusion of gold as money? *"Do you think that civilized countries have, from experience and knowledge of economics, reached a stage where they could drop the fiction, unreality, and chaotic state of a currency based on gold, and adopt a money backed by useful wealth...? This gold money...is a fiction."* — *Thomas A. Edison, quoted in TODAY, Jan. 13, 1934.*

How is this fiction transformed into a fact of painful reality? We must remember that financiers today deal in money just as most of us deal in goods, except that they need very little raw material to manufacture it. We regard the flour or coal we deal in as a commodity, and when it is scarce we know that its value will rise. Just so financiers have come to regard money which today means credit, as their commodity, and so quite logically, **they wish to keep it relatively scarce so it will command great power over goods.**

Since the value of money, as a commodity, is thus raised by limiting its supply, financiers naturally frown on any suggestion that it could be more plentiful. The supply of money is limited by the self-made rules of our existing financial system, but this fact is concealed from the public. On the contrary, the financial fraternity has placed in the public mind a deceptive illusion about the scarcity of Money.

Financial credit is restricted at the present time because money is dealt with as a commodity. So by keeping money in short supply its value as a commodity is enhanced. For this reason **it is not desirable that financial policy should be in the control of a private monopoly** whose interests are not in line with the interests of the community as a whole.

The fact that this **scarcity is a pure illusion** has been repeatedly proven. We know by the testimony of bankers that **banks create and destroy 90% of our money by bookkeeping entries** and they are dominated in this process by private gain. But because money is issued as debt and kept artificially scarce by this singular illusion, it is not available **in sufficient quantity to express the demand for goods,** which is its prime purpose.

The illusion of scarcity frustrates **the fulfillment of the purpose of money.** A constant shortage of purchasing-power is the inevitable result, and the needs and desires of us as consumers must go unsatisfied to this extent. So long as the subtle illusion of scarcity is sustained, by financial power, this scarcity will continue.

A very interesting sidelight on this situation is given by confidential circulars issued in 1877 by leading New York bankers to all national banks.

The banks were told that, *"To repeal the law enacting national bank notes or to restore to circulation the government issue of money will be to provide the people with money and therefore seriously affect your individual profits as bankers and lenders. You will at once retire one-third of your circulation and call in one-half of your loans. Be careful to make a money stringency felt among your patrons, especially among influential business men."* — Arthur Kitson, Industrial Depression.

Well, the stringency has been many times felt. We know its painful power. But it is a boomerang hastening the downfall of finance itself, to say nothing of its devastating effect upon the personal pocketbooks of the nation's shoppers.

By issuing money as a debt, the banking system can recall and destroy credit-money at will. The exercise of this power produced the panic of 1929. Deposits produced by bank creations of private money, lent as created, were contracted wholesale. This started a shrinkage in demand of bank backed loans and deposits of $20 billions of dollars. It has resulted in a reduction of the volume of check-money turnover from $1200 billions in 1929 to less than $400 billions in 1933. This amounted to an annihilation of two-thirds of the money supply for the transaction of business.

Such deliberate shrinkage of private money by the contraction of credit and bank loans and bank deposits, produced the depression of 1907. Again in May, 1920, a meeting was held in secret by members of the Federal Reserve board, the Federal Reserve Advisory Council, and 36 Class A directors of the Federal Reserve banks which are owned by the private member banks; in this meeting, after an all-day discussion, it was determined to contract the nation's credit and currency.

As a consequence, beginning in July, 1920, the commodity price level declined from 166 to 93, as compared with the price level of 1913. Agricultural products fell by more than one-half while the value of farms declined from a gross of $79 billion to $58½ billions.

12
The Monopoly Of Credit

Any attempt to portray the facts of our monetary system would be incomplete without some specific mention of the monopolistic nature of the control over Money. Let it be said plainly that we are dealing only with facts as we find them. There is much disgruntled "bank-baiting" today, and we must never let ourselves engage in that needless sport. Above all our attitude must be open-minded. But we cannot appreciate the need for a 21st Century scientific money system without knowing where the faults lie in the broken-down financial failure that now impoverishes us.

We have seen how the banks, in the process of their bookkeeping, create and destroy the money underlying our use of checks. And we have seen how more and greater debt is the necessary consequence of this bookkeeping process. We may justifiably conclude that the power of the banking system, through its functions of creating, expanding and contracting, regulating and destroying money, is without limit, unparalleled and sinister.

More than 97% of the total money owned by the individuals of the nation is privately issued, and the larger part of it has no tangible existence whatever by far. It represents a debt owed by the nation to the international bankers who own the money supply, enforceable by the law, who have (with the sanction of national authority) been quietly adding to the burdens of the nation.

President Wilson, speaking in 1916, pointed out that, *"A great industrial nation is controlled by its system of credit.*

The growth of the nation, therefore, and all of the nation's activities are in the hands of a few men who chill and destroy genuine economic freedom."

Taxation and The Money Monopoly:

If you investigate the facts as to the ownership of these world debts and war loans you will find them predominantly held by large financial institutions. You have at once a very good business reason for large quantities of taxation if half of it goes to the service of national loans which are held by large financial institutions: that as an ordinary business proposition is obvious. It is still more obvious when you consider that **these debts were created in the first place by financial institutions** loaning money to governments in return for large blocks of national securities which the financial institutions obtain for nothing.

Borrowing Our Own Credit!

We read a great deal in the newspapers about "government financing" and the "National Debt." What is the meaning of these terms? The personal witness of a government official can best explain them.

*"Some years ago I happened to be in conference with the President when the Secretary of the Treasury came in, and, with tears in his eyes, expressed doubt that a necessary loan could be floated. Then the thought came to me, what an astounding situation it is for **the Government to borrow money from banks that the banks do not have**, and then, by redepositing the money in the bank, loan the same money back to the banks, and pay them interest on it to boot. The Treasury of the United States has been largely under the control of the great*

banking houses of the country ever since the Civil War, because of the so-called National Debt."

Responsibility and Where it Rests:

Surely a great responsibility is assumed by any group of men who exercise dictatorship and control over the monetary policies of a nation. And more than that, when this dictatorship involves a monopoly over the creation and supply of money, then the administration of this power, which affects the lives of millions, is a task requiring little less than superhuman wisdom. The life of every citizen rests in the hands of those who control money. **Control of the money system means the control of civilized humanity.** Rothschild's remark: *"Permit me to issue the money of a nation and I care not who makes its laws,"* is filled with human importance.

Since money is the medium of exchange for goods, the control of money in practice means the control of Wealth itself. Moreover this control of money involves the parallel power of control over politics and business as well, affecting the economic destinies of producers and consumers alike.

Being now in a position to note the extent to which a modern industrial community depends for its well-being on a wise and disinterested money policy, we see that *the real rulers of any country are those who hold the power of money issuance and restriction.* There is an old axiom in banking and investment circles: *"It takes money to make money."*

The inevitable result of the monopoly of money is the concentration of Wealth and Power in the hands of the few private individuals who own and operate the monopoly. The monopoly of the control of the money system is the greatest monopoly in the world at the present time.

The Attitude of Common Sense:

The monopoly over money is controlled by private individuals. This fact deserves careful consideration. The private banking system has the power to create and destroy the greatest part of our money supply, but the shopping public generally does not know how its pocketbook is thusly being pinched. Our criticism is not against the creation of money, it is against the monopoly of power to create it, held by the banks.

Right here, we must understand a very important point. **We are not, in any sense, criticizing bankers as individual business men.** Above all let us keep malice out of our attitude toward this question. Knowing the facts we must appraise them wisely in order to reach a true estimate of their consequence. Let us agree therefore that bankers as individuals are by no means so inhuman as to desire the harmful effects of the system in which they work. We all know many of them, honest capable men. They are clearly not the subject of our criticism. They are the unwilling victims of the system in which they work, for the debt-formulas of the goldsmiths govern the system.

It is not necessary to assume that the bankers set out deliberately to will bad trade, unemployment, poverty, revolution, or war. Nevertheless, they will the policy that brings them about, and must, therefore, accept responsibility. Their operations are so hidden from view that the majority of the people, not being given to hunting for ultimate causes, do not connect them with their own misfortunes. But if the bankers persist in denying responsibility they must make way for men who are prepared to accept it.

It is the peculiar defects in the banking system itself that command our attention. In these defects and their consequences, through which the money-power controls every phase of our economic life, lie the main causes of our present privation and suffering. **These defects must be repaired before money can accomplish the purpose for which it is designed.**

13
The Shortage Of Buying Power Arising From Prices

So far we have dealt mainly with money. Practically all purchasing power comes into existence in the form of credit, and though it may be transmuted into cash in its passage through the hands either of poor men who have no banking account, or of rich men who require pocket-money, it resumes the form of credit to be extinguished.

We have seen that the first fundamental defect in our money system is an artificial scarcity of money resulting from the monopoly over its supply and its creation as debt. The second defect is more subtle and, if possible, even more disastrous than the first, for it concerns the direct relation of money to goods. Its pinch is felt in every purse, from beggar's to millionaire's, since it involves the prices we must pay for the goods we need to live.

It is generally agreed that our trouble is not **over-production** but **under-consumption**, which results from a chronic shortage of buying-power. We must note carefully the word "chronic" for at any given moment the amount of money in mans' pockets is — under the present money system — insufficient to buy the total output of industry.

Why is this so? Let us recall again our picture of the shopwindow through which we looked at America's great store of wealth. On our visit to the store we were impressed with the million different items offered for sale, and the part which Science plays in producing them.

As we look at the goods in this shop, we cannot help noticing the fact that every article for sale carries a price tag. Where do these prices come from? They are manufactured, just as goods are manufactured.

We find in the shop two simultaneous processes of manufacture going on together. The first of these processes is a visible stream of real goods, the articles of wealth we need and desire.

The second is an almost invisible stream of figures in the form of **prices**. And these two streams — goods and prices — flow together side by side, uniting in the shopwindow as goods for sale, with prices attached. Bearing this picture in mind let us see how prices become attached to the goods.

Buying Power and Prices:

Every factory is more than just a producer of goods. The goods it manufactures must sell at a price. And the price at which they sell must cover all the costs involved in their production. From the viewpoint of money, therefore, every factory produces not only goods but also **prices**. So that for every article of goods produced a price is produced as well.

How do we, as shoppers and consumers, get the money to equal the prices of the goods we wish to buy? In the workshop of wealth we found two streams flowing together, the first one a stream of real goods and the second, a parallel stream of prices attached to these goods. Now to complete the picture we have to add a third and last stream of money-tickets.

The stream of real goods and the stream of prices both flow out of the productive system. So also do the money-tickets with which to buy goods come to us from the productive system **as salaries, wages, dividends and**

profits, which we call the "**buying power** of the Nation."

The personal income, derived from the productive system in return for services rendered, is the only shopping fund that the nation possesses as shoppers. It is all the money that the nation as shoppers receives to cover the priced values that the nation as producers has made.

So our incomes depend on business. Naturally when the nation is busy producing we receive more money, and less when business slows down. But the most important thing that interests us is to **compare,** over any period, **the number of money-tickets trickling to the shopping nation out of industry with the price-values created in the shop, over the same period**. If the money received by *Shopping-America* were always equal to the price-values created by *Producing-America,* then we could purchase all the goods that we can produce. We might perhaps dispute about the distribution of the tickets but we would certainly have enough of them to buy our total production.

But we don't find this to be so. Experience proves that it isn't true. What we find in fact is that the buying power of the Nation, flowing from the productive system as wages and salaries and dividends, **is much LESS than the price values created in the same period**. The two streams of buying-power and prices, do not move together, either in volume, or in rate of flow. **The stream of prices to the shops flows much FASTER than the stream of shopping tickets to the shopping public.** The result is that our buying power chronically lags behind the price-values of the goods in the shop.

Now, the only permissions to go shopping, and that means to live, are the money payments distributed as buying power to shoppers. But **the money distributed amongst the**

shoppers at any time is only enough to equal about TWO-THIRDS of the price values in the shops.

That is a matter of fact and not a matter of theory. It can be proved by simple arithmetic, which was confirmed by experience in 1920, when Major Clifford H. Douglas pointed out the gap between buying power and prices. He discovered the constant lag of buying power behind prices. He has revealed to us why we are poor in the midst of plenty. He showed us the gap separating us from the wealth of goods we can produce.

In that gap between Buying-Power and Prices lies the root cause of depression, of poverty and human suffering, of strikes and riots, of bankruptcy and business failures. On one side of the gap is plenty of goods. On the other side is a chronic shortage of money.

No wonder then that there are always more goods than there are buyers! No wonder we fight each other for these precious money-tickets! No wonder everyone has to look for employment in the shop in order to live. Those who can't work in the shop have to be supported by the rest of us through relief programs and charity. And so long as the gap separates buying power and prices, permanent business recovery is hopeless.

An Everyday Example:

For example, we can easily understand this chronic shortage from an illustration showing how modern business operates. Let us consider a radio factory which has been in business for the past five years. The owner of the factory finds that his competitors are installing new labor-saving machinery, which reduces their costs below his own figures. He must have these new machines in his plant in order to continue business, He calls on his banker and asks for a loan of $10,000 to buy the necessary machines.

The banker, who considers the plan a sound one, grants the loan, incidentally creating the $10,000, which our radio producer now owes back to him. The latter hopefully buys his machinery and installs it. He finds that the new machinery will replace ten men, who are no longer needed. So he lays them off. Their place is taken by the new machinery, which costs him only its depreciation and power charges. He saves the pay of these ten men, who lose their jobs and their wages. Here is a real loss of buying power, arising out of the replacement of men by machines.

How Prices are Made:

The process of price building extends all the way from raw materials to the shop window, but we can look at a cross-section of it right here in the radio factory. The first thing we see is that every cost, **including profit**, which enters into the production of a radio must be charged into the retail price paid by the consumer. Otherwise the factory cannot keep operating. All costs, **including profit**, must be recovered in prices. That is a fundamental business principle. If the radio manufacturer fails to recover all his costs, **including profit**, he will soon be out of business.

In his operating statement which records all his costs and payments, there are two different and distinct kinds of costs. Therefore we will divide his total costs into two groups, calling the first group **"S" (Shoppers' costs)** and the second **"B" (Business costs).**

S-costs will be all the payments that the factory makes **directly to individuals**, such as wages, salaries, bonuses, dividends, and profits.

B-costs will be all the payments **made to other businesses**, for such things as raw materials, machinery, light, heat and power, insurance, taxes, bank charges, advertising expense, and all the other external costs that appear in a business operating statement.

Now all the **S-costs** are payments made directly into the hands of individual consumers, who can use them for shopping. These **S-costs** therefore represent actual and immediate **buying-power**. For the persons who receive them as salaries and wages, they are shopping tickets that can be used immediately to buy wanted goods.

But the **B-costs** are payments made to other businesses which in turn distribute them. It is of course true that eventually most of the **B-costs** will **over time** reach the hands of individual consumers, but in the radio factory which is the particular cross-section we are observing at the moment, only the **S-payments** actually reach individuals who can use them for shopping.

However, all the **S-costs** and all the **B-costs must be charged into the total selling price** of the radios if the manufacturer is to recover his total costs, plus a reasonable profit. Consequently, the total selling price of the radios he produces must include all the **S-costs** as well as all the **B-costs**. Therefore his selling price must be **S-plus-B**.

How the Shortage Arises:

Now we have an interesting picture. The only immediate **buying-power** distributed so far in the production of the radios is **S**, and obviously **S** alone is less than **S-plus-B**, which is necessarily the price. Therefore **S**, representing salaries and wages which are money payments to individual consumers, **can never buy S-plus-B** which is the price of the finished radios. It is a fact of present financial practice that industry cannot distribute enough money to consumers by wages, salaries, etc., to enable them to buy and enjoy the goods it produces.

Now when we, the shopping nation, want to buy a radio we must pay in its price all the costs involved in producing it. We pay not only for the radio but also for part of the costs of the machinery and other overhead charges of the radio factory. In fact we buy not only the radio alone, but also a part of the factory that produced it. In the radio's price, we must pay all of the costs involved in its production, but we have only the money represented by the **S-costs** to spend. That is all we receive for shopping.

So the situation under our present price system comes down to just this: **there is a chronic shortage of shopper's buying-power generated in the flow of business**. The figures of research indicate that over a given period of time, out of the total costs of industry, **the money available as purchasing-power amounts to only TWO-THIRDS of the value of the total output**. This shortage of buying-power is inherent in the process of price building.

What makes this gap between buying-power and prices?

While the fact of the gap is the important thing, the explanation of the gap offered by Major Douglas appears convincing. He says that **much of the money put into the productive system as bank loans never, in fact, gets out as income during the same period in which it is put in.** It is used simply to transfer capital goods from one factory to another, and thus while it adds to the price-stream, it does not add to the income of us shoppers.

From the shopper's point of view, retail prices come to us loaded with all the costs of production and distribution.

They include repayment of bank loans, interest, depreciation charges on plant and equipment, and all other costs of production. All these costs must be paid for in the retail price we pay to buy the goods. But against them we have available as **buying-power** only the thin trickle of shopping-tickets that reaches us as salaries, wages, dividends and profits. So the more we borrow from the banking system to produce wealth, the wider grows the gap between buying power and prices. Meanwhile debt piles up to a new high peak.

All the credit that the community gets and converts into money, and spends or saves, is manufactured by the banks out of nothing. It is lent to manufacturers, dealers, and others who require it for their business, and is circulated by them throughout the community. Some of it goes directly into the pockets of consumers, as wages, salaries, or dividends; and in being spent it transfers goods from the ultimate vendor or retailer to the consumer — that is its function. This we will call **"consumer-credit,"** and the costs it creates **"consumer-costs";** that is, costs representing purchasing-power in the consumer's hands; costs he can pay."

The rest of the credit issued is used to transfer goods, not from retailer to consumer, but from one business firm to another. This we call **"business-credit,"** and the costs it creates **"business-costs."** The distinction is purely one of function, and is made for elucidation purposes. So far as the business world is concerned it is not perceived to exist. If it was, the economic problem would probably have been solved long ago. Any bank credit will perform either function.

Business-credit, as defined, is nobody's income — that is the importance of the distinction made above — so **business-costs** are costs the consumer has no money to meet and cannot therefore pay.

Business-credits are mere replacement credits, replacing earlier issues of consumer credit which have been spent and extinguished; for what is a **consumer-cost** at one stage of the productive process becomes a **business-cost** at all subsequent stages.

The Time-lag:

But if this gap has always existed, why have we not felt it sooner? Why have the effects of the chronic lag of buying power become so apparent only recently?

The very word **sooner** points out the answer to this question. It is largely a **matter of time**. The word "chronic" comes from the Greek word meaning "time." **The flow of money in exchange for goods and services takes time.** We have been looking only at one cross-section of this flow in the radio factory. **The flow is as continuous as time itself. It never stops.** And as soon as we look beyond this cross-section, and take in a longer period of time we shall see the same thing repeated over and over again.

At every point, just as we saw in the radio factory, the "S" costs are LESS than the total **S-plus-B** prices, so that over any given period of time the total prices (**S-plus-B**) must always be greater than the total shopper's buying power (**S**). The payments of money to individual consumers who use the money for shopping **always lag behind** the prices of the goods that shoppers want to buy. The longer the time the greater the lag.

If we go back to the radio factory to the maker of its machines, we find the same situation that we saw in the radio factory itself. And if we go still further back to the foundry that made the parts of the machines and even to the mining of iron ore, it is again the same story. All along the line the amounts of money distributed by industry as buying-power are always less than the price of the finished product. At the root of this lies the factor of time. The lag of buying-power behind prices is a time-lag. Time and money taken together give us a "rate of flow of money." **The rate of flow of money payments to shoppers always lags behind the rate of flow of the price** of the goods.

All Along the Line:

At any given moment there is a shortage of the buying power necessary to equal prices. And this shortage is cumulative, it keeps growing larger. The flow of costs into price starts with the prime producer and builds up to the retail selling price which shoppers must pay for the goods they consume. These goods tend to flow through business in a straight line from the raw material producer to the consumer. It takes time to move goods from one step to the next. At every step along the line all the costs involved in this step, plus a reasonable profit, are added into the price of the goods. As shoppers we must pay the total of all these costs. But we have only the **S-payments** to spend and therefore when the goods come on the market we can never pay **S-plus-B:** the price of the goods we need. **Even if no profits are added, we are always short of buying power.**

In addition to this fact we must remember also that profits and dividends distributed are themselves BUYING POWER because they are payments to individuals who can use them to buy goods.

The importance of this lag of consumer buying power behind the flow of prices is especially noticeable when we consider the time it takes to produce and distribute any article of merchandise. For example, we may assume that a period of eight weeks is required to assemble a radio from raw materials and to complete its construction in the factory of a producer. A week later the producer sells the radio to a wholesaler. Finally after another week, the radio is sold to a retailer who is now ready to deliver it to a shopper. At every step along this ten-week line of production and distribution, salaries and wages (**S-costs**) are paid to consumers. The wages paid during the first week are spent for food, clothing and shelter during the second week, wages paid during the second week are spent during the third week and so on to the end of the ten weeks when the radio reaches the retailer. At every point along the line the wage payments (**S**) are spent soon after they are received. Yet at every step the costs (**S-plus-B**) progressively pile up and when the radio reaches the retailer most of the salaries and wages out of which it must be bought **have already been spent**. As shopper's buying-power they are no longer available. They have gone back into the bank accounts of business again where they are again divided into **S** and **B** costs. So buying-power continues to lag behind prices

If all the costs of production were traced back to their original source, it would be found that they consist of payments made to somebody or other for services rendered; so, at a first glance, it might appear that, no matter what the cost of production may be, there is always sufficient money in the community's hands to buy the whole product. That is far from being the case. What is overlooked is that the various items appearing as costs today represent payments made over a long period of time. Some were made last week, some last month, some last year, some many years ago; but to be effective as purchasing-power now — as they would have to be in order to buy today's products — every penny of those payments would have to be saved. However, **most of the money was spent as it was received** — had to be spent by the recipients in order to live — **and no longer exists as purchasing-power**; for, as we shall see later, money, or purchasing-power, is extinguished in buying goods for final use or consumption.

The Vicious Circle:

Now let us remember how money circulates through business, beginning in a bank with a loan and ending with the repayment of the loan to the bank. The radio producer in our example has borrowed $10,000 to install his new machines. This $10,000 must be paid back to the bank plus accumulated interest. The producer must recover this money by including in the price of his radios not only repayments on the loan **but also interest on the loan**. So the public has to pay more than the producer has borrowed!

Now, when the producer repays his loan, the loan goes out of existence, but that $ 10,000 is still charged in prices against the shopping public. That amount of money has been destroyed and **the shopping public is left without a corresponding buying-power**. There is no way of putting into circulation again the money represented by the loan except by another loan from the bank for **further production**. When this occurs, the whole vicious circle is once more started. Even if bank loans are renewed instead of repaid, the money payments reaching the pocketbooks of shoppers keep lagging behind the price-value of goods. What actually happens is that the money or credit received by consumers in connection with cycles of production not yet completed — that is, not yet materialized in final consumer-commodities — is taken from them via the prices charged for goods belonging to cycles which are completed.

Thus we go round and round the circle of money and over and over the path of production. **But our incomes never catch up with the prices of the goods we need and desire.** We are like squirrels in a cage — we can make the cage go round but we can't get anywhere.

The difficulty is thus two-fold. It centers in the fact that *BUYING-POWER is not in the right hands at the right time,* that is, in the hands of shoppers when they need it to buy wanted goods.

Savings and Investment:

Our plight is still more serious when we remember that all of salaries and wages cannot be used to purchase goods. Some salaries and wages must be held as savings against emergencies and inevitable old age.

Money used for investment cannot be used for consumption. Investment diverts it back into further production thus creating a new set of costs with lessened buying-power to equal them. So investment results in widening the gap between buying-power and prices.

Whatever savings we can scrape together reduce our present buying of goods for consumption. As for hoarding, hoarded dollars are idle money simply withdrawn from circulation.

The Gap is Growing:

As we have seen, the more that automatic machinery replaces men, the wider becomes the gap between buying-power and prices because salaries and wages are thus reduced, leaving other cost items proportionately increased. When we stop to realize that the gap is constantly widening as efficient machine-power rapidly replaces inefficient man-labor in doing the work of the world, it becomes evident that we are reaching the senseless absurdity of a maximum production and a minimum of consumption. Yet we wonder at the paradox of poverty in the midst of plenty!

What Keeps Business Going?

If you ask, quite naturally, how in that case are the goods ever sold at all, the answer is that there are more ways of killing a cat than choking it with butter. The gap can be artificially bridged even if it is not actually closed.

Here we find the final answer to our question — *"Why haven't we felt the gap sooner? If this chronic shortage of buying-power was always present why did its effects only become apparent in 1929?"*

To begin with, we must first recognize a fact necessary to supply the background for our understanding. Briefly, it is that in the modern economic system the industrial side is subservient to the financial or money side.

A number of artificial stimulants have enabled our ailing financial system to conceal its weakness. For instance, goods can be willfully destroyed. Or they can be practically given away under the compulsion of bankruptcy. Or they can be disposed of in return for acknowledgment of debt, that is to say, by mortgaging our future income of money-tickets. But we shall have to content ourselves with listing the chief drugs that have postponed the breakdown of finance for adequate comment on them all would require another volume in itself.

New Bank Loans to Finance Production:

The extension of so-called "credit" from the banking system furnishes the main motive power in keeping money flowing through business. Without the extension and renewal of loans, the lag in buying-power relative to prices would soon become noticeable. Naturally, as we have seen, new production distributes fresh buying-power to consumers. But it also creates additional goods beyond the reach of this purchasing-power. Eventually we get a glut of goods and insufficient buying-power in the hands of shoppers to claim them for consumption. These loans are like a drug; the more we take the more we have to take, until we pass completely into their power.

Over-Expansion in Capital Goods Industries:
Industry is engaged in the production of two kinds of goods: **consumable goods** and **non-consumable goods** (capital).

During and after the war vast sums of money borrowed from the banks were poured into the capital-goods industries, engaged in producing non-consumable goods (machinery, etc.). This production greatly increased our productive capacity. While these industries were producing rapidly, an apparent prosperity boomed. But the resulting expansion of plant and equipment (the cost of which must be recovered in prices) only widened the gap between buying power and prices. Now, with idle factories, restricted production and shrunken incomes, we are paying the price.

Sabotage and Restriction of Production:
We have already referred to the stupidity of **sabotage** and **deliberate restriction of production**. Yet in our own country these are going on every day, both in industry and

agriculture. Most obviously we see them in agriculture, where food-stuffs, cotton and other products desperately needed by millions are restricted on a vast scale. In industry, machines stand idle or are scrapped. And all this in an effort to cut production to fit a dwindling buying-power. How long can we go on destroying our real wealth instead of using it?

Business Failures, Liquidations and Bankruptcies:
Business men have swallowed a strong dose of these bitter medicines in past years. Liquidations and mark-downs on merchandise are ruinous to business. Nevertheless, by lowering prices they give a temporary increase in the buying-power of the shopping public. But the gap continues between buying-power and prices because the benefits to buying-power thus gained are counter-balanced by unemployment, the failures of banks, and similar losses caused by bankruptcy.

The Export Market:
In the past, exports absorbed much of the domestic production which American buying-power was unable to purchase. Exports are largely financed by foreign loans, once easily arranged but now increasingly difficult. Our own shortage of buying-power requires that exports increase as machines increase our productive capacity. But the possibility of exports diminishes as mounting tariff barriers, unpaid international debt, and competition between nations prevent us from dumping our surplus abroad.

Worst of all, competition for survival in the export market breeds economic conflict which is the forerunner of military war itself. As things are, one nation can only expand its foreign market at the expense of other nations; and when an expanding market is a matter of life and death, the end of the scramble is war. War in our day, whatever it may have been due to in times past, is an outcome of the efforts of industrial nations to avert **excessive unemployment**; since **excessive unemployment** endangers their existence.

"Peace? Why ... is there any man here or any woman ... who does not know that the seed of war in the modern world is industrial and commercial rivalry? The war was a commercial and industrial war. It was not a political war." — Woodrow Wilson, Sept. 1919.

One More War?

When war comes, the necessity of national preservation sets aside the old rules of finance; production has the right of way. Salaries and wages are thus distributed, but for producing armaments and munitions that are to be blown up and other goods to be consumed by the fighting forces — for goods, which never appear in the shopwindow to be sold to the shopping public. The nation pays the bill, and the buying-power of consumers, enriched by these new wages and salaries, is enabled to absorb a greater proportion of the goods that are for sale. Temporary prosperity reigns.

War cures unemployment by providing millions of men with jobs in the army and navy; while the rest of the nation is kept busy supplying them with armaments and munitions. Credit may be difficult to get in peace time; but in times of war it flows like water, ensuring plenty of money to spend. Plenty of money to spend means a ready sale of goods and rising prices; and what is not sold for peaceful consumption is blown up into the air or otherwise destroyed. Production is at a maximum; and the market never becomes overstocked.

But when the war is over, the inevitable debt to the international banking system that financed the war must be paid. The outlet for goods is once more restricted, productive capacity is greater than ever, so depression ensues.

The horrid memory of the war is still fresh in our minds. **The price of death and destruction is too high to pay for wartime prosperity.** We are told that the next war will be many times more destructive than the last. **Can any sane man look forward without a shudder to the destruction of civilization?**

How Debt Develops Depressions:

Looking over this list of futile palliatives it is easy to see that every item in this list, except perhaps sabotage, is tainted with **the disease of debt.** Altogether, they are hopeless of remedies to combat the spread of this disease. Slowly but surely the poison of debt-money infects the blood of business until the breakdown is reached and financial collapse follows the debt-disease.

To save themselves the banks are forced to sell securities and recall loans, thus cancelling credits, and destroying the very money they have created. Falling prices, business paralysis, and unemployment follow. The sequence is familiar to all of us in business. Such attempts to cope with the strains and stresses of a modern economy by a money system that is unable to sustain them is repugnant to both science and common sense.

To sum it up, business goes on despite the shortage of buying-power because it must go on. We need its goods and services in order to live. But the economic system is burdened with debt, chronically crippled by the lag of buying power behind prices. It hobbles painfully along delivering only a fraction of its potential goods and services. We pay the price of its progress in poverty and suffering. Adequate buying-power would prevent our paying this price. But we keep on paying the price of poverty because the money system as it operates in prices **is not self-liquidating**.

And the burden of debt grows heavier year by year.

From Debt To Prosperity

14

Revolution Or Evolution

So long as the present gap separates buying power and prices what good can be expected from international Peace Conferences? And what relief can be accomplished by new and greater government bond issues to finance a "relief program" based on more and bigger debts?

With increasing speed we are being driven to make a choice. Will we deliberately choose to continue in debt and poverty while we follow the past lead of Russia to a revolution of senseless violence in this country? Or will we choose instead prosperity and plenty following a necessary, orderly, and peaceful **evolution** in the bookkeeping of our money system?

This is the choice Americans must make. This choice is inevitable because our productive machinery is worse than useless unless we can use its products. Its sole purpose is to produce and deliver wanted goods and services for consumption. These wanted goods and services together with our ability to produce them, constitute our real national wealth. Furthermore this wealth is the only real basis of our National Credit.

But we cannot use that Real Credit today because the perverted bookkeeping of our broken-down money system shows it as **unpayable debt, not as a credit**. The burden of that debt will continue to paralyze business until we realize that **the Credit of the United States is a national asset**. It is only common sense and good business to show in our bookkeeping the ability **to produce as a credit, not as a**

debt to the bookkeeper. We have still the opportunity to choose. Why should we wait for another bookkeeping failure to force us into national collapse?

We have seen that a sound money system must provide circulating money, **free of debt,** as the condition of its issuance in sufficient quantity to express the effective demand for available goods. With the supply of money in the hands of men who must be interested primarily in their own profits, how can we expect money to be reasonably related to the supply of goods? A financial monopoly from which money **is born as debt** can only result in a money system that ignores the needs of consumption. It is simply common sense that such a system would result in a chronic shortage of purchasing power.

The dangerous **illusion of scarcity,** with the power it gives over human life, exists because, in the past, it has worked to the advantage of those who control Finance. Few people realize how subtly they have been involved in this deception. The world's money-masters and their paid economists have practiced their craft for so long that the illusion appears to most of us as a fact, instead of a **transparent sleight-of-hand trick,** or as Professor Soddy terms, **"le(d)gerdemain."**

The evidence is clear that so long as we tolerate the artificial **illusion of scarcity,** with which the popular idea of money has been surrounded, **Financial Credit can never be a true reflection of Real Credit**. Yet by its very nature no money can be sound unless it adequately expresses the demand of the shopping-nation for existing goods, and goods that can be produced. But so long as private people can get money created for them and destroyed again when they have done with it, money must be capricious in its value and business a game of chance.

We need hardly wonder that the monopoly over money has broken down. We might better wonder how the monopolists have been able to operate it for so long. So schooled have they been in sustaining the strategy of their illusion that they have become the victims of their own creation. It is a curious paradox that to the international banker the Wealth of a nation appears as something on which he may place a mortgage to issue money as an evidence of debt; while to the shoppers of the nation, its consumers of goods, that same Wealth represents the satisfaction of vital needs and desires. Yet freedom from poverty is frustrated by the shortage of money-tickets.

The obvious necessity for a clean-cut change is everywhere evident in the banking system. The whole financial system of this country is so stained that it cannot face a genuine inquiry. Many broad-minded bankers are aware of this fact, but Finance cannot save itself. Too many of its own executives have fallen under the hypnotic spell of the power they must wield. The necessary change in banking **must come from outside of the banking system itself**.

The Choice is Ours:

Strange as it may seem the monopoly over money exists simply because we have allowed it to continue. In terms of human suffering we know the miserable consequences of its power. Who chooses blindly to tolerate poverty? The public can close any bank it wishes to close at any time by refusing to do business with it.

An actual demonstration of this occurred in 1933, when public fear and distrust closed every bank in the country. The money-monopoly can dominate our lives only so long as we continue to allow it to do so.

But there is still a stranger fact about the private control of the supply of bank-money in circulation. While the total amount of money issued by the banks varies only in accordance with their own action in increasing or diminishing deposits, yet the Constitution of the United States explicitly provides that Congress shall have exclusive power to issue money and regulate its value:

The creation and circulation of money by the banking system is a direct usurpation of the essential prerogative of government, giving to that system paramount influence over the national well-being. The Government, in allowing the banking system to enjoy a practical monopoly of this power, has forfeited a duty which now it must resume. In the present abundance of goods the **artificial illusion of the scarcity of money** is a prime cause of human misery. **And we ourselves as citizens and taxpayers are responsible for this situation.**

The time has come for the Government to assert its constitutional right to control the issue of money for the benefit of every citizen. If we want business recovery we can get it only by closing the gap between buying power and prices. We can do this either by reducing prices or by increasing buying power until the two are equivalent. But the most effective method to close that gap is to **raise buying-power** and to **lower prices at the same time**.

To accomplish the raising of buying power and the lowering of prices clearly necessitates a change in our broken-down money system. **What we require is a supply of credit correlated with our supply of goods at all times.** The monopoly of credit can no longer continue to issue money only as debt.

The first immediate necessity is to restore to the nation the right to control its own money system. The Constitution grants this power to Congress, as the elected representatives of the people. The assertion of this power is the first step in the direction of permanent business recovery and freedom from our slavery to the money monopoly.

The time for the change has come. It is here and now. The overwhelming forces of economic necessity require that we face this fact, and give our earnest attention to the design and operation of a money system that is sound, that will equate our buying power with the supply of goods we can produce. To refuse this challenge is nothing less than national suicide, as we have seen.

From Debt To Prosperity

15
Social Credit Proposals

Social Credit meets this challenge. The solution to this, the greatest problem of our day, provides a scientific money system by basing the supply of credit directly upon the supply of goods. **Social Credit is the ability to monetize our existing real wealth for the benefit of society.** Social Credit gives mankind a definite and practical plan for the control and use of this money system, designed specifically to overcome the chronic shortage of buying power.

The business of a modern and effective financial system is to issue credit to the consumer, up to the limit of the productive capacity of the producer, so that either the consumer's real demand is satiated, or the producer's capacity is exhausted, whichever happens first.

Moreover Social Credit aims directly to jump-start an immediate and permanent business recovery. Its object is to cease the accumulation of national and international debts, and to put an end to the continual and simultaneous existence of chronic poverty and glut.

With growing certainty the voice of the shopping public demands that the deluge of debt be replaced by individual security. Depression must give way to lasting national prosperity solidly founded upon Real Wealth. In this Age of Plenty, brought about by our progress in scientific achievement, we have already learned that every consumer is a partner of industry. Production cannot go on without constant buyers.

We have seen that the present shortage of buying power in the hands of consumers is due to two fundamental causes, both of them rooted in the system of Debt-money. The proposals of Social Credit are designed to remedy these causes and to **eliminate the shortage of purchasing-power**. What we are aiming at in the Social Credit Movement is to increase purchasing-power so that the money system shall become self-liquidating, and to meet that condition, fewer and fewer operators will be needed to tap the machines of industrial production.

This may sound like a large order. Let us see how it is to be filled. Social Credit says that it is as possible as it is logical and necessary.

To claim that a world which has witnessed the marvelous mechanical, scientific and cultural progress of the past 150 or so years cannot reform a combination of accounting and ticket-issuing functions so that they truly reflect the physical facts as they change from time to time, is to ask too much of the credulity of an exasperated public, for it simply is not so.

16
The National Credit Account

If we want money to work for us instead of against us we must use **Credit-money** instead of **Debt-money**. We can only enable the economic system to deliver wanted and needed goods and services by closing the gap between buying power and prices. As more debt-financed relief programs fail to bridge this gap the necessity for action becomes increasingly plain. Equally obvious should be the fact that the most effective method to close the gap is to raise buying power and lower prices at the same time.

But how can this be done in practical operation? It is self-evident that any lasting and general prosperity depends upon maintaining a constant balance between a high rate of production and an equally high level of consumption. This balance results from continuously satisfying the vital needs of consumers with the actual physical goods of producers. To make their demand for goods effective consumers must have sufficient money to buy the goods. Demand, without money to implement it, is impotent, ineffective. **The only actual limit to the satisfaction of the shopping nation's need for goods should be the limit of our productive capacity**, of which we are now utilizing only a small fraction.

Therefore sufficient money must be available to accurately express the demand for wanted goods. **Money, being the bridge between desire and goods, must depend upon our Real-Credit**; that is to say, the rate at which we as a nation can deliver the goods and services we require to live. Real-credit is the capacity of a community to deliver goods and services as, when, and where required throughout the world.

In other words, money must reflect the true facts of the world's Real-Wealth. Since money is the accepted means to express the effective demand for available goods, the balance between our ability to produce and our ability to buy and consume what is produced must be accomplished by money.

Permanent business recovery requires then that we level up consumption to balance with production. The nation as shoppers and consumers of goods must be able to buy what we produce. If **America as shopper** is to buy the output of **America as producer** we must begin to raise consumption up to the level of productive capacity.

This can be accomplished only by controlling the total amount of money in circulation so that it will be increased or expanded at exactly the same rate as production and consumption are increased. Only in this way can the balance between production and consumption be maintained, and the desires of consumers for goods be satisfied in permanent prosperity.

A money system that is sound, that delivers wanted goods to shoppers for consumption, must be a true expression of Real-Credit. Furthermore **Financial-Credit must be fully equal to this Real-Credit,** otherwise money cannot reflect the true facts of our Real Wealth. The re-identification of Real-Credit with Financial-Credit is the vital issue.

What Must be Done:

Two things are necessary to make the money system reflect our Real-Credit. And both things must be done by the government of the United States, acting as the representative of the people of the world. Both can easily be done by existing governmental agencies.

We have seen that the first necessity is to restore to the nation its Constitutional right to control our own money system. The government must exercise its sovereign power to control the nation's money supply. This includes credit as well as currency. This action is the first requirement for permanent business recovery.

Second, the government must gather together the facts and figures of our ability to produce and deliver useful wanted goods for consumption. As we have seen, our Real-Credit rests upon this solid foundation.

Once the nation regains constitutional control of its own money system, the immediate practical step proposed by Social Credit is to appoint a non-political **Federal Credit Commission**. As its primary duty this Commission would take a national inventory of our actual productive capacity for wanted goods. Based on this capacity to produce wealth a **National Credit Account** would be established in the United States Treasury.

The **National Credit Account** is simply a business statement showing the known facts of our ability to produce wealth in goods compared with our ability to buy those goods to consume them. This **National Credit Account** provides the practical means *by which the government can monetize the nation's Real Wealth,* that is, to express its value in money. The purpose of this Account is to keep the **price-values** created in the nation's workshop of wealth in constant balance with the **money-tickets** distributed for shopping. Its object is to provide a constant supply of credit correlated exactly with our supply of goods.

Social Credit proposes to supply the money necessary to level up the balance between production and consumption by means of the **National Credit Account**. This money will be created as credit by the Government, acting through the United States Treasury. The money itself will be **sound money** in every sense of the word, for its value will be based upon the **Real-Credit of the United States.**

Monetizing our Real-Wealth means the transformation of our vast present Real-Credit into its financial equivalent. This is necessarily a bookkeeping operation, exactly like the present creation of money. But Social Credit requires that instead of the nation's money supply being created in the bookkeeping of the private banking system **as debt**, it would be created in the bookkeeping of the United States Treasury **as credit.**

How to Do It:

The non-political **Federal Credit Commission** would gather together and show in a national balance sheet all the facts of our enormous productive capacity as compared with our present limited, restricted consumption of goods. The nation would be **credited** with its production of wealth and **charged** with its consumption. This balance sheet would show the real limit of the National-Credit. By means of this business-like method, **the surplus of production over consumption would be made available as credit to increase consumption.**

Sufficient money in the form of credit would then be issued by the Treasury **direct to consumers** to enable them to buy all the wanted goods produced. This **credit-money** will be exactly sufficient in quantity to enable our established productive capacity to deliver goods and services to shoppers for consumption. The amount of the money must therefore be based on the current relationship between production and consumption.

In essence, the **National Credit Account** is simply a **statement of the facts of the nation's business, of the production and consumption of Real Wealth, over a given period**, reflecting the truth of our Real-Credit. This Real-Credit is transformed into Financial-Credit in the bookkeeping of the United States Treasury by the Constitutional power of the Government.

The administration of the **National Credit Account** would be the duty of the **Federal Credit Commission**, a non-political body of commissioners comparable in authority in the realm of business to the Supreme Court in law. The members of this commission would be appointed by the President, by and with the consent of the Senate, to serve for a definite term of office. The membership of the commission would change in rotation as seven year terms of office expire. The commission could not be politically influenced because its work would deal only with the facts of production and consumption. No more than four of the commissioners could be members of the same political party.

But we must understand clearly the most important point to be grasped about this controlled issuance of credit-money based on the Real Credit of the nation. **The money thus created is backed 100% by the Wealth of the nation, its ability to produce and deliver wanted goods and services.** Credit, convertible into money, is a correct estimate of the capacity of society to deliver goods and services desired by individuals. This Wealth, created by the industries of the nation, is a **true Asset.** Social Credit recognizes this wealth as an added national value, a true asset, **not as a debt to the banking system.**

A rough example in round numbers will illustrate in a general way how the **National Credit Account** provides the facts necessary to monetizing our Real Wealth:

(SEE FOLLOWING PAGE)

In terms of this example, based on the Real Credit of the United States, the Treasury could issue $25 Billion dollars in **Credit-Money**, thus transforming this Real-Credit into Financial-Credit available to consumers for shopping.

Banks and Bankers - An Important Necessity:

The institution and keeping of the **National Credit Account does not require any "nationalization" of the banks.** As a matter of fact, such nationalization would be a great mistake. Only **Monetary Policy** need be under national control. The present banking system could just as efficiently carry out a policy for the national benefit as it carries out policies for its own private profit today.

"I am not myself, for instance, an advocate of the nationalization of banks. I believe this again to be one of those misapprehensions so common in regard to these matters, for the nationalization of banks is merely an administrative change: it does not mean a change in policy, and a mere administrative change cannot be expected to produce any result whatever in regard to this matter. A change in monetary policy can be made without interfering with the administration or ownership of a single bank in the world." — Speech by Major Clifford H. Douglas, at Oslo, Norway, 1935.

At quarterely intervals, the Federal Credit Commission would submit the following statement of Real Credit to the U.S. Treasury — **NATIONAL CREDIT ACCOUNT** (figures in billions of dollars)

Credit = Additions to Real Wealth	Debt = Subtractions from Real Wealth
1. PRODUCTION (a) Shoppers goods ------- 70 (b) Capital goods ------- 25 2. Imports ------- 3 (Real Wealth received) 3. Appreciation ------- 2 (Increase in commercial capitalized value of operating assets) 4. Payments on Foreign Debts ------- ? (Received from other nations)	1. CONSUMPTION ------- 60 (Shopper's goods at retail including National Dividend spent) 2. Exports ------- 6 (Real Wealth sent abroad) 3. Depreciation ------- 9 (Wear and tear on plants, business equipment, etc.) 4. Payments on National Debt ------- ? (Spent to retire bonds held by banks, reduce Taxation, etc.)
Total ADDITION to Real Wealth ------- 100 (Enrichment)	Total SUBSTRACTION from Real Wealth ------ 75 (Impoverishment)

REAL CREDIT BALANCE ------- 25 } Available to finance additionnal consumption.
(Surplus Net Enrichment of Real Wealth) (By means of Discount and Dividend)

(These figures are merely illustrative, not factual)

While Social Credit would do away with the monopoly over the **supply** of money as now maintained by the banking system, it would preserve banks and protect bankers. The government would assume, as its proper Constitutional function, full authority for the supply of money. But this change does not imply any violence, nor does it contemplate putting the banks out of business. As proposed, Social Credit in the United States would save the banking system for private ownership.

The banks would operate under the supervision of the Government as agencies of the Treasury. They would handle money, accept deposits and carry on the bookkeeping necessary to the use of checks and the transaction of business. In fact the bank as repositories of the people's money and as efficient collectors of debt, are most useful institutions, and banking is one of the fine arts of the modern world. The machinery of the banks should as far as possible be retained — perhaps extended — although **monetary policy** should be withdrawn from private control.

This simply means that the banks would no longer hold the **Monopoly-Power** to create and destroy money as they do today. Business and individuals alike need the facilities of the banking system to carry on their activities. All the useful functions of banking must be preserved for the service and convenience of business. But the banking system would also be the means through which the government dispenses money and credit to consumers. Bank loans as a service to business would be backed by "cash on hand" as credit, not created "out of nothing" as a debt. Fees for service rendered would be the bankers' recompense instead of interest on money created as debt.

The Social Credit proposals would require and reward

the ability of every capable and public-spirited banker, since their function as bookkeepers and agents of the **National Credit Authority** is still required to be carried on. The opportunities of bankers for rendering valuable and profitable service to the public would multiply as increasing prosperity is achieved.

The **National Credit Account**, reflecting our Real Wealth and equating Financial Credit with Real Credit, would provide sufficient circulating **credit-money** for business and consumers. The practical operation of the **National Credit Account** means the transfer of the control of credit from the banking system to the government as the representative of all its citizen-consumers.

No confusion or discarding of present business practice need attend the introduction of the **National Credit Account**. In fact the first steps in this direction have already been taken by the Government, through its purchase of bank stocks for the purpose of operating the **Deposit Insurance Plan**. The government has used its authority to determine the eligibility of banks for participation in this plan. This is in reality the beginning of widespread recognition of the necessity for Government control of monetary policy, even though, in a strange paradox, the **Deposit Insurance Plan** was necessary to bolster up public confidence in our present inadequate banking system.

Public opinion will bring pressure to bear when enough of us realize that **artificial scarcity continues** and the present shortage of buying power is increased because self-made methods of the banking system restrict our supply of money. When the facts are known, public demand will change this situation.

Is it not absurd that banks continue to **monopolize money and credit** only by our government's consent?

The Government is empowered by the Constitution to issue and control the value of money. Why should it not be forced to exercise this right? Yet we not only allow the banking system to continue its monopoly, but even the government itself borrows its own credit, piling up an increasing burden of public debt owed and payable to the banks!

A Guarantee Against Inflation:

The suggestion that the government create money to be issued as buying power to the nation's shoppers may cause some people to fear "inflation", as a result. This word inflation is one which is always raised by bankers and those whose interests are with bankers, when any question of modification to the money system is raised.

The first thing to realize is the true meaning of inflation. **Inflation is not an increase of purchasing power,** it is an increase in the number or amount of money-tickets, whether paper or otherwise, accompanied by an increase in prices, so that both the **money-to-spend side** is in figures raised and the **price side** is also in figures raised. That is true inflation.

It is common knowledge that inflation is dangerous because it is characterized by rising prices, ruinous to the buying power of wage earners. But Social Credit would avoid and prevent inflation by automatically controlling the money supply, **not only in its issuance** but in relation to the wealth in goods against which it is issued. The amount of money issued through the **National Credit Account** would be so regulated as to avoid both inflation and deflation.

The panics, crashes and depressions of the past would no longer threaten the security of our economic life. Social Credit would positively insure the direct control of money in relation to goods — a relative stability of prices and values — by means of a Just-Price.

The Twofold Use of Consumer Credit:

The money created on the basis of the **National Credit Account** would be used in **two ways** to close the gap between buying power and prices, to overcome the present shortage of purchasing power. **The first way** is called the **Just-Price** that is designed to increase the buying-power of every shopper's dollar while preventing the inflation of prices. **The second way** is called the **National Dividend**.

Let us consider first the Just-Price.

From Debt To Prosperity

17

The Just-Price

The **"Just-Price"** is the pivot of a sound economic system, balancing the outward and inward flow of credit with the production and consumption of goods; and it cannot be determined by haggling in the market, the present method of determining prices. It is a matter for scientific calculation based on recorded statistics and a simple computation.

More Buying-Power for Everyone:

As soon as the **National Credit Account** makes our Real-Credit available for use, the second step necessary for permanent business recovery is to establish a **scientific pricing system** designed to apply this credit where it is most needed. This pricing system must operate specifically to close the gap between the Nation's present insufficient trickle of **shopping-tickets** and the **price-value** of the goods in the shop.

Business survival demands that all costs must be recovered in prices. We know that to buy goods shoppers must present their **shopping-tickets** or establish credit in the store of wealth. It is here that the total cost of production and distribution is collected from the shopping public. **The logical way to increase buying power and at the same time to lower prices is to bring New Money into existence as a Discount on the retail prices of goods and services.**

By this discount on retail prices Social Credit proposes to lower prices and increase buying-power. The Just Price is simply the **regular retail price minus this Discount. The Discount would apply on all goods sold to shoppers at retail for consumption.**

The Retailer is the point of contact between business and the consumer, the last link in the chain of distribution connecting production with consumption. Accordingly the retail price must include all the costs of production and distribution and whatever profits are to be made. The total of all these costs and profits is the **Retail Price**. Hence it is here, at this final point, that the balance between production and consumption must center.

The adoption of the Just-Price would raise the purchasing power of every shopper by establishing a continuous **retail discount** on all retail purchases. The object of Price regulation (at the Just-Price) is to put an end forever to the alternating recurrence of inflation, when credit is said to be plentiful; and deflation, when credit is said to be scarce. By means of the Just-Price, industry will be able to receive a proportion of its costs of production from the **National Credit Account**, so that industry will no longer depend wholly on the **inadequate purchasing power** that it now distributes to consumers.

To balance the money payments which consumers receive from business with the total retail price of the goods offered for sale, a Retail Discount would be extended to all shoppers and consumers of goods.

How The Discount Would Work:

This may sound complicated in practice so let us apply it to our everyday experience and illustrate its operation. For example, suppose we have been for a long time wanting to buy a new tire for the family Ford. But we have postponed our purchase for lack of cash. The retail price of the tire is $100. The retail discount rate at the time is 25%. Now applying a discount of 25% to the retail price of $100 would give us a Just-Price of $75. With the extra buying power which the discount gives us we go to the tire dealer and buy our $100 tire for $75.

At first thought, the idea of buying a $100 tire at less than cost may seem surprising. It is certainly a bargain for us. But it works to the tire dealer's advantage too. Let us follow the handling of this translation to see how it works. The sales clerk who sold us the tire records the sale, showing on his usual sales slip the retail price and also the amount of discount that has been allowed us.

The retailer then follows his usual practice of depositing his receipts in his bank. But he includes together with them a **discount voucher** showing all his transactions and the total discount allowed on all of them. The bank then credits the **retailer's bank account** with the total retail value of all his transactions, thus giving him the **total retail price**, recovering all his costs, and enabling him to balance his books.

The bank in turn reports to the U. S. Treasury the total amount of the discount it has disbursed. The discount is charged against the debit side of the **National Credit Account** as consumption. The bank is repaid with **Treasury Credit Certificates**, thus balancing its books.

What is the net result of this bookkeeping process? The retailer's books balance, the bank's books balance, and the **National Credit Account**, by this simple procedure, raises the buying power of all of us, balancing consumption with production. The whole process is in fact less complicated than many business methods already in common use. That its results would add to our buying-power hardly needs to be pointed out.

Where does the money come from to finance this increase in buying power? It is created by a bookkeeping process **exactly as it is now created by bookkeeping.** But it is derived directly from the Real-Credit figures shown in the **National Credit Account**, instead of from the debt figures of the private banking system.

We have seen that in the **National Credit Account** the shopping nation is credited with the full production of Wealth and charged for their consumption.

The production of Real-Wealth must necessarily always run ahead of consumption. The Retail-Discount is determined by the difference between the actual production of Wealth and its actual consumption. So the credit to finance the discount thus comes **from monetizing the surplus of production over consumption** as shown in the **National Credit Account.** The bookkeeping creation of this credit grows out of the excess of **Real-Credit production** over **Real-Credit consumption.**

Real Cost - and Why:

The Just-Price is based on Real-Cost — on the principle that the true cost of any article is the total of all that is consumed in producing it.

If we make a Table, for instance, a certain amount of wood is consumed, a tree has been cut down somewhere in the forest; there has also been a certain amount of depreciation in the saws, logging tools, freight cars, machinery in the mill and factory, and so on down to the truck that finally delivers the Table to our home. At the same time other products such as food and clothing, have been consumed by those engaged in cutting down the tree, sawing it into lumber and making the Table. At the end of the whole process the tree, the food, and all the rest, have been partly or wholly used up; and the Table is left. Now what has it cost us? Obviously the total of the things consumed in making it.

In the same way, if we look at our total production of goods for any given period of time, we can say that its real cost has been our total consumption over that same period of time. And if production has exceeded consumption, then in terms of Real Wealth we show a net profit on our work. Our Real-Credit has increased.

The Just-Price (the retail price less the Discount) is based on the fact that **the real cost of Production is Consumption.** If we momentarily disregard the financial aspect of Industry and concern ourselves with goods only, it becomes clear that the actual physical cost of things produced is the material used up and machinery worn out in the making of the things. What does a community gain during any given period? New factories, new processes, development of mines, and goods of every kind, manufactured or imported — in other words, **new capacity to supply men's needs,** new Real-Wealth. What does the community lose during that period? Plants worn out, machinery scrapped, mines worked out, and goods consumed or exported. The community gains **Appreciation of Real-Wealth** at the cost of **Depreciation**, and, as we know well, **the production of Real-Wealth is ever greater than the simultaneous consumption thereof.**

But we know that all the many fixed charges on capital investment, interest, repayment of loans and other financial costs must enter into the **total retail price** of every article. A moment's thought will show us that the Real-Cost of any finished article will always be less than its Financial-Cost. Social Credit proposes that by means of the Just-Price consumers should pay the Real-Cost (that which is consumed in real-wealth), and that the remaining balance of the total retail price should be represented by the Discount. The function of the Discount is to overcome for consumers the difference between Real-Cost and Financial-Cost, to bridge the gap between **buying-power and price.**

All social advance is held back by the amount of consumer's income; and since the **buying-power and price** are not equal, a mere trickle of good reaches him. If any change is to take place, if the trickle is to become a flow proportionate to the productive power potentially present, **the consumer's income must be increased**; but the increase must come **from somewhere outside of the productive system**; it must not appear **anywhere as a cost** or costs will rise in proportion to the consumer's income being increased, and no more goods will reach him. In other words, it must be a **free issue** of money.

What We Pay For in Prices:

As we saw in the radio factory, industry produces not only goods, but also prices. And we found that the shoppers who bought a radio paid in the price not only for the radio alone but also for a share of the factory that produced it.

So, all goods produced under the present method of price-building must sell at a price that includes not only the direct-cost of each article but the cost of the means of production as well. All the financial costs involved must be recovered as well as the real-cost.

When we consumers buy a sack of flour, we also have to pay part of the cost of the railroad that transported the wheat and the mill that ground it into flour. To be sure we consume only the flour, we have no appetite for railroads and mills. But after we have eaten the flour in our daily bread, the railroad and the mill which we have helped to pay for still remain. And in them the capacity to deliver more flour still remains.

When we buy goods we buy what we want to consume. Yet under the present price system, we pay not only for what we consume but also for factories, workshops and machinery, which we cannot consume. And after we have consumed the goods we buy, the factories and machinery still exist, ready to produce surplus goods which we cannot consume.

The purpose of the Just-Price (which is based on Real-Cost) is to enable us to pay as we go for what we actually consume. Social Credit rightly regards the means of production as useful assets. It is false accounting to regard new money created by a bank at interest, for the production of wealth, as a debt against the shopping nation to be recovered in prices. Honest bookkeeping would credit the nation with the value of the new capital assets, on the strength of whose resources the money was created.

Our capital plant and equipment for production is a part of our Real-Wealth. When we pay for the means of production we are buying what we cannot and do not consume. Social Credit insists that in the Just-Price we pay for what we do consume. The other costs involved in retail prices are met with the **national Retail-Discount**.

So we see that the term **"Just-Price"** is not merely a phrase. We are applying the actual facts of production and consumption to the prices we pay for goods and services. The Just-Price is a logical and convenient way to conform the business accounting to our ever-lagging buying power.

When we consider the many complex discounts which play so large a part in every business today, it becomes evident that a uniform discount on the retail price of all goods sold for consumption would be easy to record and control. The Just-Price involves no changes in our present efficient business structure, no futile attempts at price-fixing, no Government interference with business.

Consumer Control of Credit:

The Just-Price would put the control of how credit is used **into the hands of consumers themselves**, for the discount applies only to sales actually made.

The credit working in the discount as increased buying power **is issued only when goods are sold** so the relationship of goods and money remains the same, constant. Thus Social Credit prevents the inevitable inflation and collapse that follow the expansion of money under the present system of money as debt.

New money, under this plan, comes into circulation as the result of people spending money on something they need and want. If goods remain unsold, there is no reimbursement to retailers, and no new money is issued to them in that regard.

The new money issued, far from raising the general level of prices, actually lowers the general level of prices, and is in no sense of the word inflationary. Most other proposals for increasing the **purchasing-power** of the public entail an issue of new money and some device to prevent the natural tendency of prices to rise. The issue of new money is itself the device whereby prices are in fact reduced to their proper level.

Nor would any speculation be possible in the use of this credit, for it would be applied to specific goods at the moment of sale.

Since the Retail-Discount would reduce the price of all consumers goods **it would make an actual addition to the buying-power of every dollar of our income**. For example, at a 25% discount $4000 worth of goods could be bought with an income of $3000 dollars a year. The discount would provide extra buying power which we could use in any way we wish. The Retail-Discount thus adds to shoppers income and reduces the prices of the goods in the shop, effectively closing the gap that now breeds poverty, depression and war.

Yet the Just-Price would destroy neither profits nor competition. On the contrary, by causing a greater turnover of goods the Just-Price would stimulate business. Competition would encourage an adequate purchasing-power instead of a deficient one as at present.

Selling under cost in the way described would not deprive anyone of a dime of his income. The adjustment in prices corrects a flaw in the financial bookkeeping which keeps prices above incomes and so hinders the distribution of goods. There is no question of penalizing anybody or making him poor; that is quite unnecessary. The whole object is to make *everybody* well off, not just a few.

How The Just Price is Determined:

In considering the many advantages of the Just-Price we must remember that the amount of Retail-Discount at any particular time would be determined by the existing facts of production (new plants and imports) and consumption (including depreciation and exports). These facts are itemized in the National Credit Account. The Just-Price is then determined by the mathematical ratio between the total **production of wealth** and the total **consumption of wealth**. In terms of the previous example, the Retail-Discount would be calculated as follows:

$$\frac{\text{Net Real Credit Balance}}{\text{Total Additions to Real Wealth}} = \frac{25}{100} = \frac{1}{4} = 25\% \text{ Discount}$$

The current quarterly rate of Retail-Discount would then be 25%.

National Dividends are also paid out of the **National Credit Account**. As explained earlier the total of **National Dividends** paid would be added to consumption since the Dividend would be used for consumption.

For the benefit of those scientifically inclined, the following formula is used for arriving at the Just Price:

$$\frac{\text{Financial Cost}}{\text{Of All Goods Produced}} \times \frac{\text{Goods consumed}}{\text{Goods produced}} = \frac{\text{Just Price}}{\text{Retail Price}}$$
less Discount

Social Credit proposes to put the Just-Price into effect thus adding to our buying power and reducing prices. It is suggested that we would start with a very conservative discount of 15% on all retail purchases to be consumed. This initial discount rate, however, would not be permanent but in the future would vary periodically in accordance with the facts of production and consumption.

For example, after a three month period of operation at a discount of 15%, during the next three months period the discount might be fixed at 20%. In the following period actual production figures would be used to calculate the discount. Thus business would pick up gradually and surely. We would then have accurate reliable data to determine the discount just as the insurance companies base their rates on actuarial statistics. The rate of discount would then be revised quarterly, as the **National Credit Account** records changes in the relationship of production and consumption.

From a business viewpoint the Just-Price coincides with current business practices. The procedure for accounting and recording the discount is familiar to every accountant. Every business would agree to a specified rate of profit on turnover to prevent profiteering, and together with price competition would limit any tendency to raise prices. Any retailer who tried to take undue advantage of the increased purchasing-power of consumers would forfeit his right to dispense the discount which would leave him at the mercy of his competitors; cheating simply would not pay.

Business Recovery:

In practical operation the Just-Price would furnish immediate relief from the present depression, by starting the wheels of industry turning to supply the new goods called forth by this increase in shopper's buying-power. And by applying the whole amount of the discount against retail purchases for consumption, we would soon consume the "unsalable surplus" that exists today. No longer would we destroy cotton, pigs, and other useful wealth that we had sweated to produce, nor let our factories stand idle while their products are wanted.

The industrial system has never functioned at more than 25% of its productive capacity, having been hampered by the defective purchasing-power of a debt-burdened and over-charged body of consumers.

This immediate relief would be still further stimulated by a psychological factor. As consumers, we should hasten to promptly take advantage of the discount, for in advance of its quarterly revision we should not know how much increased business might cause the discount to diminish in the next quarter.

To visualize the effects of the Just-Price, we need only ask ourselves "What would I do with a dependable 20% increase in my income?" We would put the money to use immediately to buy goods. And that buying would start America's workshop of wealth to producing and delivering more goods. As shoppers we could buy all the wanted goods in the shopwindow. Business would begin to move forward and grow again. The economic system could fulfill its function of supplying the nation's shoppers with wanted goods and services for consumption. The Just-Price provides the sound business basis for permanent recovery.

The natural tendency of any civilized nation that possesses the advantages of machine-power production is to grow richer and richer as new Real-Wealth is produced. In any modern community appreciation far exceeds depreciation. Ultimately commodities cannot for any length of time be consumed faster than they are made, and capital appreciation (new factories, new machinery and the development of mines, etc.) continually outstrips capital depreciation. Even — one might almost say — especially — during the late war, productive capacity was enormously increased, while ultimate commodities were replaced as fast as they were consumed or destroyed.

But because our false bookkeeping requires that **we monetize our wealth as debt to the banks**, this flaw in the money system makes us poorer and poorer instead of increasingly more wealthy. The consequences of such stupid ignorance are filled with human suffering. The adoption of the Just-Price would end this human suffering at once by making prices reflect the facts of our production and consumption of Real-Wealth.

We can only liquidate the crushing burden of debt that now paralyzes industrial activity by making payments against it out of the profits resulting from increased business. Years of prosperity are required to accomplish this but the Just Price provides the most practical means for its achievement.

Much as the Just-Price would accomplish to end depression and debt, obviously its advantages could not be enjoyed by those who have no money at all to spend. What then of the unemployed? The pick-up in business would unquestionably provide employment for most of them, but what of the rest?

Social Credit meets the problem of unemployed for everyone, with the National-Dividend as already explained.

From Debt To Prosperity

18
About Clifford Hugh Douglas
The genius who discovered Social Credit

Clifford Hugh Douglas
1879-1952

In regard to the birth of Social Credit, there is one name, the name of a man of genius, a Scot: Clifford Hugh Douglas, born in 1879, son of Hugh Douglas and Louisa Horfdern. Graduated from Cambridge University, with an honour degree in mathematics, Douglas chose to be an engineer by profession.

He was a brilliant engineer, who was entrusted with important projects. He was, in India, Chief Engineer and Manager for the British Westinghouse Company; in South America, Deputy Chief Electrical Engineer for the Buenos Aires and Pacific Railway; back in England, he was employed on the construction of the London Post Office Tube Railway; then, during World War I, he was Assistant Superintendent at the Royal Aircraft Factory in Farnborough, England. After the war, he ran a small yacht-building yard, in which he was helped by Mrs. Douglas, who was herself an engineer.

Douglas was also an expert in cost price accounting. It is for this expertise that the British Government asked him to go to Farnborough in 1916 to sort out "a certain amount of muddle" in the Aircraft Factory's accounts.

Douglas never bore the title of economist; he would have considered this as an insult anyway because of the monument of errors, based on false premises, in economic teaching in universities. Yet, Douglas was actually the greatest economist of all times, with his diagnosis of the major flaw in today's economics, and with the proposals he formulated to solve it.

Throughout his career as an engineer, Douglas had to tackle problems of physical nature and solve them. But he gradually noticed that, if the solving of physical problems was always possible, many enterprises were stopped because of purely financial problems. That led him to study the financial question with the spirit of an engineer.

He briefly related himself, in an address to members of the Canadian Club in Ottawa, in 1923, how he came to take interest in the question of finance and credit. The report of this address was published in the April 15, 1923 issue of the Ottawa Citizen.

Douglas said that his first experience with financial hindrances stopping physical possibilities, dated back about fifteen years earlier, around 1908. At that time, he was in India, in charge of the Westinghouse interests. He had to conduct a survey, at the insistence of the Government of India, of a large district with considerable water power. He found a large amount of exploitable water power, went back to Calcutta and Simla to report it, and asked what was going to be done about it. The answer was: "Well, we have got no money."

Douglas found that decision deplorable. For this was at a time when the manufacturers in Great Britain were finding it hard to obtain orders, and the prices for machinery were very low. As for India, it badly needed electric power. But "they had got no money", and Douglas could only accept it, while pigeonholing in his mind this case of a beautiful physical possibility that was paralyzed by a financial impossibility.

Round about that time, he said, he dined frequently with J. C. E. Branson, the Controller General in India. This Branson used to bore him considerably by discussing something he called "credit". Treasury officials in India and Britain persisted in melting down and re-coining rupees (India's coins), having regard to what they called the "quantity theory of money". Yet, insisted Branson, silver and gold had nothing to do with the situation; it nearly entirely depended upon credit. Douglas subsequently remarked that had he be given a short lecture on Mesopotamia, it would have been, at that time, just as unintelligible. But, nevertheless, Branson's repeated words had also been pigeonholed in Douglas's mind.

Just before World War I, Douglas was employed by the British Government to build a railway for the Post Office from Paddington to White Chapel. There was no physical difficulty at all with the enterprise. He was ordered to get on with the job. Suddenly, he got the order to suspend work and pay off the men. Always for the same reason: no money.

Some time after that, during the war, he was sent to the Farnborough Royal Aircraft Works, to sort out a muddle which the books of that institution had gotten into. It was not long before that he had remarked that, each week, the cost prices of the goods produced were greater than the income distributed in the form of wages and salaries. Prices were not in accordance with purchasing power.

All that drew his attention, and a study of the cases of many companies showed him that it was so in every factory. How could, in those conditions, the money distributed to consumers buy the products? Douglas also remarked that once the war came, there was no more a question of a lack of money. So there was nothing sacred with money. Money could appear all of a sudden, and *all that is physically possible can be made financially possible,* as it was the case during the war.

Douglas also faced other experiences. He decided to locate and up-date the defects of the financial system; then, as an engineer, to seek, discover, and formulate principles to put finance in keeping with the reality of the times. This is what has been called since Social Credit.

Douglas first published his conclusion in an article in the English Review for December of 1918 under the heading "The Delusion of Super-Production", and then a series of articles of A. R. Orage's weekly review, the *New Age.* Those articles were reprinted in 1920 as *Economic Democracy,* Douglas's first book. The same year appeared Douglas's *Credit-Power and Democracy,* then *Social Credit* in 1923, *Control and Distribution of Production* and *The Monopoly of Credit,* both in 1931, and *Warning Democracy* and *The Alberta Experiment,* both in 1937.

Apart from these books, Douglas also travelled the world to give lectures on Social Credit — to Canada, Australia, New Zealand, Japan, and Norway. In 1923, he gave evidence before the Canadian Banking Inquiry, and in 1930 before the MacMillan Committee on Finance and Industry, in England.

Douglas died in his home in Fearnan, Scotland, on September 29, 1952 — the feast of Saint Michael the Archangel. He was 73.

From Debt To Prosperity

19
Economic Security For All

There have been times in the history of the world when some event or discovery has enabled the human race to take a great step forward. Major Douglas's discovery is of this type. It brings economic emancipation within our reach, if we can free our minds sufficiently from economic superstitions to understand and grasp what is offered.

"What are we trying to get? What are we aiming at? We are endeavouring to bring to birth a New Civilization. We are doing something which really extends far beyond the confines of a change in the financial system. We are hoping by various means, chiefly financial, to enable the community to definitely step out of one type of civilization into another type of civilization, and the first and basic requirement of that, as we see it, is Absolute Economic Security." — C. H. Douglas, An Outline of Social Credit, pp.46-47.

In considering the Retail-Discount and the National Dividend, we have noted some of the many advantages contained in each. But before leaving them we must understand that **both the Just-Price and the National Dividend are inseparably linked together in a constructive economic program.** The importance of this coordinated functioning of the two cannot be overstated.

Both must operate together. The Just-Price equates purchasing-power with total retail prices, prevents inflation and stabilizes price levels. The National-Dividend supplies buying-power to those of us who have none at present. **The two are conjoined in purpose, in operation, and in effect.**

Our everyday experience proves that the outworn financial formulas of the past can never again be made to provide a lasting prosperity. It is unthinkable that we can find the way out by burying ourselves under new and higher mountains of debt. The way out is not through more debt, **it is through the use of our REAL-CREDIT.**

The knowledge of what Social Credit is and how it will provide Economic Security is imperative to every intelligent American today. The issuance of National-Credit direct to consumers, based on America's Real-Wealth, is our greatest single necessity. How long must the **artificial illusion of scarcity** stand between our physical needs and the Real-Wealth that is ours? The opportunity to grasp prosperity is here at hand; we must take it now, or be regimented in poverty.

The reform suggested is not put forward as an alternative to Capitalism, but as an alternative to Chaos. So long as the present system can provide the majority of people with a living of some sort, no alternative, however attractive, has much chance of being considered. But if it becomes obvious that the system is breaking down — and the manifest difficulty of providing employment and doing profitable business are two of the evidences that it is breaking-down — *the only alternative that has a chance of being successful is the one that can reconcile the greatest number of interests with the minimum of disturbance.* The

Social Credit proposals of Major Douglas fulfill these conditions. Their title to general support is that *they can make the poor rich without making the rich poor,* and involve no change in administ-ration, only a change in financial policy.

Of the present world crisis Major Douglas has written:

"The breakdown of the present financial and social system is certain.... A comparatively short period will probably serve to decide whether we are to master the mighty economic and social machine that we have created, or whether it is to master us; **and during that period a small impetus from a body of men who know what to do and how to do it,** *may make the difference between yet one more retreat into the Dark Ages, or the emergence into the full light of a day of such splendor as we can at present only dimly envisage."*

This book has only presented in a general way the major principles of Social Credit. We have given little more than an outline of the practical application of these proposals to prices and purchasing power. We have not even touched upon how the Just-Price and National-Dividends would enrich our personal lives. Indeed that would require a book in itself.

This book is only a first step toward the understanding of what national action is necessary to achieve economic security in the United States.

America is the richest nation in the world. We can

produce Wealth in abundance; but Money is scarce.

To move goods from producers to the hands of consumers money must be as abundant as our Wealth.

Most money is Credit — we cannot deal in Wealth without Credit. Real-Credit, based on Wealth itself, is the soundest foundation for money. Social Credit says: "Monetize our Real-Wealth — make Financial-Credit match Real-Credit." Then we can satisfy the needs of our people with the wealth we can produce.

There is no excuse for poverty when we can produce enough wealth for all. Anything that is Physically possible is Financially possible. It only takes common sense.

Social Credit is sound and practical. It is based on methods already in use in business.

Social Credit guarantees business recovery, a new era of lasting prosperity for Americans and the people of the world. Social Credit will reduce Taxes and liquidate Debt. It will Abolish Poverty and Prevent War.

Social Credit is not Socialism or Fascism. It is not based on state ownership or state control of production. It involves no confiscation or redistribution of existing wealth but would provide instead more wealth for all of us based on our ability to produce that wealth.

Social Credit stands for the American principles of individual initiative, freedom and liberty. It is opposed to financial or any other sort of dictatorship. Major Douglas says "Systems were made for men, and not men for Systems; and the interest of man, which is self-development, is above all systems, whether theological, political, or economic." —*Clifford H. Douglas, Economic Democracy.*

Social Credit does not advocate the nationalization of the banks. Social Credit would save the banking system from total collapse. But it would require the nation to utilize its sovereign power to issue money and regulate the value thereof, while the banks co-operate with the Treasury and the distributive agencies of credit, receiving their recompense by service fees.

As said above:

Social Credit provides the only known means for increasing buying-power and at the same time preventing inflation. When the hypnotic spell of **the illusion of money-scarcity** begins to lose its hold over awakening Americans, the servitude of man to money will at last be abolished and economic security for all will become a fact.

From Debt To Prosperity

20
Guernsey's Monetary Experiment

by Louis Even

Guernsey is a small island located in the English Channel. An Anglo-Norman population. This island is located closer to the French coast than to the English coast.

At the close of the Napoleonic wars, the island, like several countries, was in pitiful condition, both physically and financially.

No money:

Sea walls, roads, and markets were needed. There was no manpower shortage, but there was no money to pay for these works.

The money used by the people on the island was the money from England, the pound sterling. But, *like after any war,* the financiers were calling back the money advanced to finance the slaughter, and the pounds sterling were very scarce, everywhere.

The island had an autonomous government, "the States of Guernsey." So it had the rights inherent in all sovereign governments, among other rights, that of regulating the volume of money in circulation in the country. But, no more than any other country, the States of Guernsey had not thought of exercising this sovereign prerogative.

An intelligent governor:

The island was especially in need of a new market house, and a committee was set up to take care of it. The committee went to see the governor to explain the situation to him: "We need a new market, but we have no money to build it," they said.

"With what material are you going to build a market?" asked the governor.

"With stone and wood."

"Do you have it in the island?"

"Certainly, and in plenty."

"Do you have workers?"

"Yes again. But it is money that is lacking."

"Could not your Parliament issue money?" asked the governor.

A new idea!

This idea had never occurred to the committeemen, who had never analyzed the money question. They knew where to get money, when there was some available: but they never wondered where money can begin or begins.

The method of taxing, when there was money, was quite familiar. But the method of issuing money that is lacking, and of taxing, only if necessary afterward, was something new to their administrators.

Issues of national currency:

From Debt To Prosperity

An estimate of the cost was prepared and the States printed the money required, which was paid to those who either worked on the project or furnished materials for it.

As the new currency was paid out into circulation among the people, exchanges were being expedited. The wage-earners went to the shopkeepers, the shopkeepers went to the producers, the producers bought enough to increase their production.

This currency was accepted everywhere. The government took measures against inflation by decreeing that money would be withdrawn, by taxes, so it would not accumulate. And in fact the money was retired by taxes on schedule. But, as the increasing activity required a corresponding volume of money, other issues were brought out by the government for other works.

Two years later, on October 12, 1822, the new Market house was completed and opened. Not a penny of public debt on this public enterprise was spent.

The bankers intervene:

At the time of the original issue, there was no bank upon the island. This explains, without doubt, why there was no opposition to the issue of State money.

But ten years after the first issue, the island had become so prosperous, thanks to the activity allowed by a sufficient volume of money, that the banks of England had an eye on this island.

English bankers set up branches in the island and brought the population around to orthodox banking rules. They said, "It was unsound to let the government finance its enterprises without going into debt."

The bankers did everything they could to stop further issues from being introduced into the their system of interest-bearing loans to the government, and to withdraw from the island the interest free State money that had been paid out into circulation.

There was some resistance, but the bankers won their point, with their usual methods. **On October 9, 1836, the States of Guernsey abdicated their sovereign prerogative over the control of the volume of money.** From then on, the amount of the national currency decreased gradually, and was replaced by money issued by private bankers in the form of loans, placing the island into debt.

Nevertheless, there is still about 40,000 pounds sterling ($200,000) of national currency outstanding at this date in the island. (According to Gertrude M. Coogan in *Money Creators*, published in 1935.)

Why a financial problem?

With natural resources, workers, and a bit of common sense, there is no financial problem.

But when shrewd exploiters want to regulate economic activities according to their power and their profit, there the financial problem arises.

Of course, minds in search of arguments to justify the present regime will say that Guernsey was only an insignificant, small island; that the control of the volume of money by the representatives of the people is good for a small country, but not for a large country.

All right. Take note of what these gentlemen object to today. These same gentlemen will tell you that the money problem cannot be solved properly in a small territory or a province, but must be brought to a federal or even to an international level!

It was not total Social Credit, yet the main issue of Guernsey, from 1820 to 1836, was a non-debt-bearing national currency, issued in accordance with all possibilities ahead of the needs.

The issues of national currency by the States of Guernsey caused neither inflation nor idleness. These issues created activity and prosperity. And these issues did not make slaves, so the bankers intervened.

Louis Even

This article was published in the January-February, 2004 issue of the "Michael Journal".

Note
Consider This:

When war broke out in 1939, the Government, which had been short of money for the past ten years, went to the banks to take out a first loan of $200 million dollars.

The banks did not have any more money on that day than they had the day before. For the past ten years, the population had been lacking money. When one is lacking money, one hardly has any surplus to store in the bank.

Nevertheless, the banks loaned $200 million dollars to the Government that day. They **wrote** $200 million dollars to the Government's credit in bookkeeping money.

And the young people, who had been wandering about aimlessly for years, because there was no money, were called immediately into action by the Government, dressed from head to toe in the Government's finest, lodged, fed, equipped, and transported to Europe to take part in the Slaughter

And this was seen in all the countries of the world.

The world had suffered from unemployment for ten years due to the scarcity of money. Yet this same world was able to fight a very costly war, because the banks created all the bookkeeping money that was needed to finance that war.

Money for War! *No-money,* for Peace . . .

21
Forbidden Prosperity

Written in 1940 by Louis Even

The gold standard was abolished in England in the first days of the first world war.

According to the Financiers, a tight-money policy is a good thing in ordinary times, to keep man from living, but when money is needed to kill, the means are found for that.

The first World War, being over, the gold master demanded the return of the Idol's Reign (the gold standard). It was deemed necessary to return to scarce money, to a drastic decrease of money in circulation.

This was the work of Montagu Norman, who became the governor of the Bank of England, in 1919. He immediately started a policy of Deflation.

The result was that as early as 1923, there were three million unemployed workers in England, ten times more than in 1920. Then after that, there was a 40% salary decrease, poverty, discontentment; ferments of revolutions and 30,000 suicides.

During these four years, the London Bankers imposed heavier blows on England than the Germans did during the four years of World War I.

The same in-humane policy was taking place on the European continent, with similar economic ruin and financial plunder, in Germany, France, Italy, Russia, and Spain.

During that time, Austria astonished its foreign visitors

with its prosperity and the contentment of the population.

After the war, reconstruction was necessary in Austria, as in all the other countries. But the Austrian Government had its own way of financing the reconstruction. Instead of borrowing from the banks and repaying them at interest, with taxes, **the Government issued debt-free money directly to the merchants provided that they reduce their selling prices accordingly.**

It was a compensation to the merchants for a price decrease to the consumers. It was to directly finance consumption by a Compensated Discount, as advocated by the Social Credit technique.

As a result, a remarkable development in industry and commerce took place with virtually no unemployment in Austria. The workers of Vienna lived in model homes. Taxes had been reduced to a minimum. There was an abundance of products at low prices.

Here is what Colonel Repington wrote in his book, *After the War,* during this period:

> "New machinery is being employed, and on the farms, prize stock is being bought and farm buildings are being improved. From Upper and Lower Austria, Styria, and the Tyrol, it is all the same story of new developments, and what is really going on is an endeavor to make the new Austria less dependent on its neighbors, and less forced to buy abroad in markets made fearfully dear by the exchange."

What did the Money Masters of London and Paris do in the presence of such remarkable results? Do you think that they said: "It is wonderful! Let's do the same thing in England and in France!"

No way! Instead they exclaimed: "This is not allowed! A vanquished nation that treats itself to such a comfort, when victorious nations wallow in poverty and are starving! This must immediately be stopped!"

And the Money Masters cracked down harder on Austria. They required the payment of the war indemnities and balancing the budget.

We know that indemnities can be paid only in kind by the exportation of products to the creditors.

Now, the victorious nations did not want to accept Austria's products, since such importation would have increased unemployment for their nationals. It was therefore impossible to supply the required reparations.

Austria was finally obliged to put its case before the League of Nations. The finance committee of this institution, made up of orthodox members of the same calibre of its Chairman, Sir Arthur Selter, **recommended an international loan to Austria to enable it to pay its reparations — but not in kind — in interest-bearing borrowed funds instead.**

The creditor countries, instead of financing their own citizens, provided Austria with the money that Austria had to refund to them with interest!

But in return for this so-called "favor," Austria was forced to open its national finances to inspection and supervision. It was obliged to establish a Central Bank after a model approved by the governors of the central banks of England and France.

Austria did not have the strength to resist the pressures. It was the beginning of a policy of Deflations with its trial of suffering and privation.

22

To Solve The Problem Of Poverty

by Louis Even

There are a lot of good things in our country, but many individuals and families who need these goods lack the right to have them, **the permission to get them.** Is there anything lacking but money? What is lacking, apart from the purchasing power to make the products go from stores to homes?

Money begins somewhere:

But then where does money begin, the money that we lack in order to buy the goods that are not lacking?

The first **wrong idea** that we keep alive in our minds, without actually realizing it, is that there is one fixed quantity of money and that it cannot be changed; as if it were the sun, or the weather, or the rain. This idea is fatefully wrong! If there is money at all, it is because it was made by someone somewhere. If there is not more money, it is because those who made it did not make more.

Another prevalent belief about the origin of money is that the Government makes it. This is also incorrect. The Government does not create money today, and complains continuously about not having enough. If the Government were the source of money, it would not have sat around idly for ten years because of the lack of money. And there would not be a multi-billion dollars National Debt.

The Government takes, and borrows, but it does not create money. Our standard of living, in a country where money is lacking, is not regulated by the volume of goods produced, but by the amount of money at our disposal to buy these goods. So those who control the volume of money, control our standard of living. *"Those who control money and credit have become the Masters of our lives. No one dare breathe against their will."* (*Pius XI, Encyclical Letter Quadragesimo Anno*).

Two kinds of money

There are at present two kinds of money: one we call *pocket money,* made of metal or paper; and the other we shall call *book money,* made of figures in a ledger.

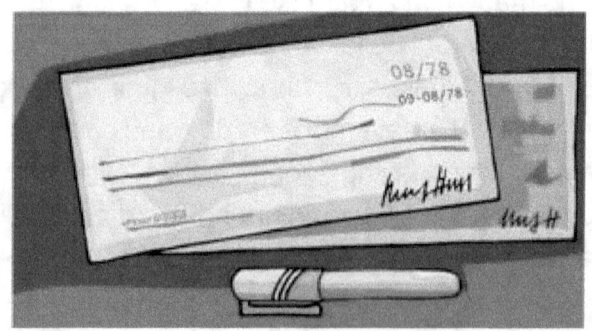

From Debt To Prosperity

Pocket-money is the *least* important; book money is the *most* important. Book-money is the bank account. Business operates through bank accounts.

Whether pocket-money circulates or not depends on the state of business. But business does not depend upon pocket-money; it is kept going by the bank accounts of businessmen.

With a bank account, one makes payments or purchases without using metal nor paper money. One buys with figures.

Let us suppose I have a bank account of $40,000. I buy a car worth $10,000. I make my payment by a check. The car dealer endorses the check, and deposits it at his bank.

The banker then makes changes in two accounts: first, that of the car dealer, which he *increases* by $10,000; then mine, which he *decreases* by $10,000.

The car dealer had $500,000 — he now has $510,000 written in his bank account.

I had $40,000 in mine — my bank account now shows $30,000.

Paper money did not move in the country because of this deal. I simply gave some figures to the car dealer. I paid with figures.

More than nine-tenths of all business is done this way. It is book-money, the money made of figures, which is modern money; it is the most abundant money; its volume is ten times that of paper or metal money.

It is a superior type of money, since it gives wings to the other. It is the safest kind of money, the one that no one can steal.

Savings and borrowings:

Book-money, like the other type of money, has a beginning.

Since book-money is a bank account, it comes into existence when a bank account is opened without money decreasing anywhere, neither in another bank account nor in anyone's pocket.

The amount in a bank account can be increased in two ways: by saving and by borrowing.

There are other ways, but they can be classified under borrowing.

The savings account is a transformation of money. I bring along some pocket-money to the banker; he increases my account by this amount.

I no longer have that pocket-money; I have book money at my disposal instead.

I can get back pocket-money by decreasing the amount of book money in my account. It is a simple transformation of money.

But since we are trying to find out how money comes into existence, the savings account, being a simple transformation of money, is of no interest to us here.

The borrowing (or loan) account is the account lent by the banker to a borrower.

Let us suppose I am a businessman. I want to set up a new factory. All I need is money.

I go to a bank and borrow $100,000 under security. The banker makes me sign a **promise to pay** back the amount with interest. Then he lends me the $100,000.

Is he going to hand me the $100,000 in paper money? No. I do not want it. First, it is too risky. Furthermore, I am a businessman who buys things at different and widely separated places through the medium of checks.

What I want is a bank account of $100,000 which will make it easier for me to carry on business. The banker will therefore lend me **an account** of $100,000.

He will credit my account with $100,000, just as if I had brought that amount to the bank. But I did not bring it; I came to get it.

Is it a savings account, set up by me? No, it is a **borrowing account** made by the banker himself, for me.

Money creators:

This account of $100,000 was made, not by me, but by the banker. How did he make it? Did the amount of money in the bank decrease when the banker lent me $100,000?

Well, let us ask the banker:

— Mr. Banker, have you any less money in your vault after having lent me $100,000?

— I haven't gone into my vault.

— Have other people's accounts been reduced?

— They remain exactly as they were.

— Then what was decreased in the bank?

— Nothing was decreased.

— Yet my account has been increased. From where did the money you lent me come?

— It didn't come from anywhere.

— Where was it when I came into the bank?

— It didn't exist.

— And now that it is in my account, it exists. So we can say that it was created.

— Certainly.

— Who created it, and how?

— I did, with my pen and a drop of ink when I inscribed $100,000 to your credit, at your request.

— Then you create money?

— The banks create book money, the money of figures.

That's the modern money that puts into circulation the other type of money by keeping business on the move.

The banker manufactures money, ledger money, when he lends accounts to borrowers, individuals, or governments.

When I leave the bank, there will exist in this country a new source of checks, one that did not exist before. The total amount of all accounts in the country was increased by $100,000.

With this new money, I will pay the workers, buy materials and machinery — in short, build my new factory.

Who, then, creates money? — The bankers!

Money destroyers:

The bankers, and the bankers alone, make this kind of money: script or bank money, the money that keeps business moving.

But they do not give away the money they create. They lend it.

They lend it for a certain period of time, after which it must be returned to them. The bankers must be repaid.

The bankers claim interest on this money that they have created.

In my case, the banker will probably demand $10,000 from me in interest, all at once. He will withhold it from the loan, and I will leave the bank with $90,000 in my account, having signed a promise to repay $100,000 in one year's time.

In building my factory, I will pay my men, buy things, and

thus spread my bank account of $90,000 throughout the country.

But within a year, I must, through the profits I make selling my goods for more than they cost me, build my account up to no less than $100,000.

At the end of the year, I will pay back the loan by making out a check for $100,000 on my account.

The banker will then debit my account by $100,000, therefore taking from me this $100,000 I have drawn from the country by selling my goods.

He will not put this money into the account of anyone. No one will be able to draw checks on this $100,000. It is dead money.

Borrowing gives birth to money. Repayment brings about its extinction.

The bankers bring money into existence when they make a loan. The bankers extinguish money when they are repaid.

The bankers are therefore also destroyers of money.

And the system so operates that **the repayment must be greater than the original loan;** the death figures must exceed the birth figures; the **destruction of money** must exceed the **creation of money.**

This seems impossible, and collectively, *it is!* If I succeed, someone else must go bankrupt, because, *all together, we are not able to repay more money than has been made.*

The bankers create nothing but the capital sum. No one creates what is necessary to make up the interest, because no one but the bankers creates money.

And yet, the bankers demand both capital and interest. Such a system cannot hold out except by a continuous and ever-increasing flow of loans.

Hence the system of debts, and the strengthening of the dominating power of the banks.

The National Debt:

The Government does not create money.

When the Government can no longer tax nor borrow from individuals, due to the scarcity of money, it borrows from the banks.

The operation takes place exactly like mine. As a guarantee pledging the whole country.

The promise to pay back is the *debenture* [a debt secured only by the debtor's earning power].

The loan of the money is an account made by a pen and some ink.

And the country's population finds itself collectively indebted for a production that collectively it made itself!

It is the case in war production. It is the case also in peacetime production: roads, bridges, waterworks, schools, churches, etc.

The monetary defect:

The situation comes down to this inconceivable thing: ***all the money in circulation comes only from the banks.***

Even metal and paper money comes into circulation only if it has been released by the banks.

Now, the banks put money into circulation only by lending it out at interest.

This means that all the money in circulation comes from the banks and must be returned to the banks someday, increased with the interest.

The banks remain the *owners* of the money. We are only the *borrowers*.

If some manage to hang on to their money for a long period of time, or even permanently, others are incapable of fulfilling their financial commitments.

A multiplicity of bankruptcies, both for individuals and companies, mortgage upon mortgage, and an ever-increasing public debt, are the natural fruits of such a system.

Decline and degradation:

This way of making the country's money, by forcing governments and individuals into debt, establishes a real dictatorship over governments and individuals alike.

The sovereign Government has become a signatory of debts to a small group of private profiteers.

A government official, who represents millions of men, women and children, authorizes unpayable debts.

The bankers, who represent a clique interested only in profit and power, manufacture the country's money.

This is one striking aspect of the degeneration of power of which Pope Pius XI spoke: governments have surrendered their noble functions and have become the servants of private interests.

As for individuals, the scarcity of money develops a mentality of vultures and wolves.

In front of plenty, only those who have money, the too scarce symbol of goods, have the right to draw on that plenty.

Hence the competition: the tyranny of the "boss"; domestic strife, etc.

A small number of people preys upon all the others.

The great mass of the people groans; many in the most degrading poverty.

The social control of money:

It is Saint Louis, King of France, who said: "The first duty of a king is to coin money when it is necessary for the sound economic life of his subjects."

Book-money is a good modern invention that should be retained.

But instead of it proceeding from a private pen, in the form of a debt, those figures, which serve as money, should come from the pen of a national organism in the form of money destined to serve the people.

One must stop suffering from privations when there is everything needed in the country to bring comfort into every home.

The amount of money should be measured according to the demand of the consumers for possible and useful goods.

It is therefore the producers and consumers as a whole, the whole of society, which, in producing goods in front of needs, should determine the amount of new money that an organism, acting in the name of society, should put into circulation from time to time, in accordance with the country's developments.

Thus the people would recover their right to live full lives in accordance with the country's resources and the great possibilities of modern production.

Who owns the new money?

Money should therefore be put into circulation according to the rate of production and as the needs of distribution dictate.

To whom does this new money belong when it comes into circulation in the country? This money belongs to the citizens themselves.

It does not belong to the Government, which is not the owner of the country, but only the protector of the common good; nor does it belong to the accountants of the national monetary organism: like judges, they carry out a social function and are paid, according to law, by society for their services.

To which citizens? To all.

This money is not a salary. It is new money injected into the public domain, so that the people, as consumers, may obtain goods already made and already funded, which are waiting for only sufficient purchasing-power for them to be produced.

There is no other way, in all fairness, of putting this new money into circulation than by distributing it equally among all citizens without exception.

Such a sharing also makes it possible to derive the maximum benefit from the money, since it reaches into every corner of the land.

Whenever it might become necessary to increase the supply of money in a country, each man, woman and child, regardless of age, would thus get his or her share of the **new stage of progress** that makes the new money necessary.

This is not payment for a job done, but a **dividend** to each one for his share in the common capital. If there is private property, there is also *community property* that all possess in the same way.

Result: order restored:

What, according to us, would be the effect of this financial reform?

First of all, in a general way, order would be restored in the money sector, consequently in economics, with echoes in the political and social spheres.

Goods would be made to serve needs.

The accumulation of money would stop being the commanding aim of industry. (And one would therefore not need to create artificial needs to sell useless products, thus reducing waste and pollution.)

The way to obtain the implementation of an honest money system is to form a public opinion sufficiently enlightened and motivated to make a successful demand for it.

So there is no question of an *election campaign,* but rather of an *education campaign.*

This propagation of study among the masses requires the devoted efforts of numerous apostles who are not afraid of self-abnegation and sacrifice.

And it is still in order.

The present disorder is the result of all kinds of selfishness. All this must be expiated and corrected.

As Pope John Paul II put it in his encyclical letter *Sollicitudo Rei Socialis:* "These attitudes and 'structures of sin' (love of money and power) are only conquered — presupposing the help of divine grace — by a diametrically opposed attitude: a commitment to the good of one's neighbor." (n. 38)

So, the surest and only way of advancing the cause of honest money is that method which develops study and devotion. This is the method advocated by the Pilgrims of St. Michael, with the "Michael" Journal. Come to our meetings, order leaflets like this one to distribute around you, solicit subscriptions to the "Michael" Journal!

Louis Even

This article was published in the May-June-July, 2002 issue of "Michael", and is also available in the form of an 8-page leaflet.

23

Louis Even - Biographical Notes

1885 - 1974

Louis Even was born on March 23, 1885, on the "La Poulanière" farm, in Montfort-sur-Meu, a municipality 30 kilometres west of Rennes, in Brittany, France. This municipality was also the birthplace of Saint Louis-Marie Grignion de Montfort. Louis Even inherited his great devotion to Mary from this illustrious patron saint. He became a fervent propagandist of the Rosary throughout his 89 years upon earth.

Louis Even was the fourteenth child (out of sixteen) of Pierre Even and Marguerite Vitre. At home, he received a sound Christian education. His elementary studies were made at the school of the village.

On August 4, 1896, at the age of 11, he entered the juvenile school of the Brothers of Christian Instruction, in Livré.

On February 2, 1901, he began his novitiate in Ploërmel. In July of the same year, an antireligious campaign began raging in France, with the enforcement of the Association Law, which restricted the activities of religious communities. Then in 1903, the Brothers of Christian Instruction were notified by the French Government that they had to dissolve their Institute. Henceforth, it was forbidden in France for the Brothers to wear the religious habit and to teach.

In Canada:

The Brothers decided to send their best students on a mission. Louis Even was part of the group. He left France for Canada in February of 1903. From there, he was sent to teach the Indians of the Rocky Mountains, in Montana, U.S.A. He stayed there until 1906. This allowed him to acquire a perfect knowledge of the English language, which was to be enormously useful to him later on when he would study Social Credit in the books of Major Clifford H. Douglas.

Louis Even returned to Canada for good on June 24, 1906, the feast day of St. John the Baptist, the patron saint of the French Canadians. That same year, he taught at Grand Mère, Que. From 1907 to 1911, he was a teacher at St. Francis' School, in Montreal.

Then he became deaf and could not teach to children anymore. He was sent to Laprairie, at the Brothers' printing shop, which was very primitive at the time. Being hard-working and very brilliant, he developed the printing shop and expanded it considerably. He acquired new machines, and to learn their workings, he had to study German, since the manuals for the machines were in German. He also studied Latin on his own. This apprenticeship of printing was to be very precious to him later on for the foundation of his Movement.

Providentially (because he was deaf and could no longer teach children), he quit the community of the Brothers of Christian Instruction where he had acquired a sound religious and intellectual formation, for he was a man of study and reflection, always having a book in his hand. He was well prepared to carry out in the world the mission that God had destined for him. He was released from his vows on November 20, 1920.

Garden City Press:

Immediately, he was employed in Ste. Anne de Bellevue, west of Montreal, at Garden City Press, a printing shop owned by J. J. Harpell, a Catholic of Irish descent. There too, Louis Even left an indelible mark of his genius on the firm.

On December 10, 1921, Louis Even married Laura Leblanc, and fathered four children: François, now a lawyer; Gemma, a teacher; Rose-Marie, a teacher and a secretary; and Agnès, a teacher. Being in charge of a family himself, it helped him to better understand the financial problems of the working-class families.

J. J. Harpell was more than just a businessman: he wanted to promote the intellectual development and general knowledge of his employees, by having them attend evening classes. In Louis Even, Harpell had found the priceless master who could make him realize his aspirations. Louis Even worked as a typographer, a proofreader, and a foreman. He translated into French the periodical *The Instructor* — the organ of J. J. Harpell's Gardenvale study circle. He trained new workers, and he was the teacher for the employees' evening classes.

Social Credit:

One day, in 1934, right in the middle of the Depression, Mr. Fielding, then Minister of Finance in Mackenzie King's Liberal Government in Ottawa, said to Mr. Harpell, who was a close friend of his: "If you want to know where the financial power lies in Canada, look towards the banks and the insurance companies."

Then Messrs. Harpell and Even decided that the evening classes for the next fall would revolve around the study of money and credit. They set about immediately, trying to find out a book on the subject. They received several books and manuscripts; one of them was I. A. Caldwell's book, <M>*Money, What Is It?*, which was later translated into French by Louis Even. But it was a simple 96-page booklet that brought him the light he was looking for. It was entitled: *From Debt to Prosperity,* by J. Crate Larkin, of Buffalo. It was a summary of Major Douglas's monetary doctrine — "Social Credit."

"Here is a light upon my way," said Louis Even. He then got all of Douglas's books, plus books of other authors on the same topic. He recognized in Social Credit a whole series of principles which, once applied, would make a perfect monetary system and put an end to the Depression. Immediately, he said to himself: "Everybody must know this." From then on he only thought about the means of realizing this wish.

The contacts established with *The Instructor* (and its French-language version, *Le Moniteur*), had given birth to new study circles, affiliated with that of Gardenvale, all over Quebec; in Sherbrooke, Quebec City, Trois-Rivieres, and Shawinigan. At the request of these new study circles, Mr. Even went to give them lectures. He naturally spoke to them about Social Credit. Then he held public meetings across the Provinces of Quebec, Ontario, and New Brunswick.

Louis Even translated into French the brochure *From Debt to Prosperity.* He also wrote articles on Social Credit in *Le Moniteur,* which was sent to some 1,200 French-speaking subscribers across Quebec, New Brunswick, Ontario, and the Prairie Provinces.

In August of 1936, Louis Even founded another periodical, the *Cahiers du Crédit Social* (literally, *Social Credit Brochures*), which he wrote up during the evenings, still working at Garden City Press during the day, and he held conferences here and there in the region on weekends. From October of 1936 to August of 1939, a total of 16 issues of the *Cahiers du Crédit Social* were published, for 2,400 subscribers.

It was during this same period that Louis Even published his great brochure, *Salvation Island* (now entitled *The Money Myth Exploded),* which he would sell for a nickel a piece to the audience after his conferences. As of today, this brochure (also published in the form of a 16-page leaflet) still remains the A.B.C. of Social Credit, for beginners. It now circulates throughout the world, by the millions, in seven different languages (English, French, Italian, Spanish, German, Portuguese, and Polish).

After a life of complete devotion to the service of God and neighbor, Louis Even passed away at 89, on September 27, 1974. Louis Even was the man who changed the course of our lives. Social Credit is a light for us all, But the life of the great Louis Even should also be a light for us all as well.

In 1946, Mr. Even published his marvellous book, *Sous le Signe dl l'Abondance.* The implementation of the principles expressed in this book would give peace and justice to the world, as wanted by God

Then in 1953, to reach the English-speaking world, Lous Even founded a journal in English, which was at first called *Social Credit,* and then, *The Union of Electors.* From 1968 to 1973, it was also called *Vers Demain,* like its French counterpart. Finally, 1974, its title was changed to *Michael,* and it is still published under this title, every two months.

In 1996, after being published for fifty years in French, Louis Even's book, *Sous le Signe dl l'Abondance,* was finally translated into English, under the title, *In this Age of Plenty: A New Conception Of Economics: Social Credit.*

This book talks about Social Credit, but it is far from being a general survey of Social Credit. Social Credit is actually a whole orientation of civilization, and deals with its social and political, as well as its economic, aspects.

We believe that, with Clifford Douglas — to whom the world owes this enlightening doctrine — that putting right the economic order along Social Credit lines, is impossible without first putting right the political order.

The title of this book — *In This Age Of Plenty* — clearly shows that we are not dealing with an economy of plenty in which access to the huge possibilities of modern production is made easier for all.

24
An Example Of Banking Philosophy

To seize the belongings of all nations and individuals.
— This is the real reason for poverty in the world . . .

In reading the following article by Louis Even, first published in 1941, one will quickly realize that the plan of the Financiers to seize the people's wealth and the farmers' land has been going on now for a long time. But today, one can clearly see that this plan has been fully realized. The people owe all of their country's wealth to the Bankers through national debts, and a majority of the farmers of developed countries have disappeared; those remaining must work night and day to pay interests to the Bankers. Let us all read again this important document that enlightens us all on the real reasons for poverty in the world.

by Louis Even

Commentaries are unnecessary on text that speaks for itself. We now have in our possession **three documents** relative to the crisis of 1893.

1. **An 1891 document:** the confidential leaflet of the bankers, encouraging mortgages on properties, in anticipation of the crisis that the bankers would launch later on to grab all of the mortgaged properties. Here is the text:

"We are authorizing our loan officers from the Western States to loan on properties, monies repayable by

September 1st, 1894. No fatal date is to exceed this date.

"On September 1st, 1894, we shall categorically refuse all loan renewals. On that day, we shall demand the repayment of our money, under penalty of foreclosure on collaterals.

"The mortgaged properties will become ours. (Money will have become scarce beforehand, and the repayments will have become generally impossible.) We'll thus be able to acquire, at a price agreeable to us, two-thirds of the farms west of the Mississippi and thousands more east of this great river.

"We'll even be able to possess three quarters of the western farms as well as all the money in the country. The farmers will then become land tenants only, just like in England."

2. **An 1892 document:** in which the Bankers expose their philosophy in an article published by bankers in the *United States Bankers' Magazine* in 1892, re-published in the *New Era* and in the *Social Creditor,* where we took it:

"We must go forward cautiously and consolidate each acquired position, because already the inferior social stratum of society is giving unceasing signs of agitation. Therefore, prudence dictates to us a line of conduct that seems to give in to the will of the people, until the execution of our plans be well-enough established for us to be able to declare our intentions without having to fear any organized resistance.

"Our confidence men shall have to closely watch the Farmers Alliance and the Knights of Work, and take steps immediately, either to control both associations in accordance with our interests, or to break them.

"Our men will have to attend the Convention that will be held in Omaha on the 4th of July, and be in charge of all activities. Otherwise, this Convention could muster such an antagonism to our plans that we would have to resort to force to overcome it.

"Now, at the present time, using violence would be premature. We are not yet ready to confront such an assault. Money must first of all seek maximum protection in schemes and in legislation.

"Let us make use of the courts. Let us go forward as fast as possible at perceiving debts, at foreclosing (depriving of recourse to justice when a certain time limit has been transgressed) on debentures and mortgages.

"When, through the law's intervention, the common people shall have lost their homes, they will be more easy to control and more easy to govern, and they shall not be able to resist the strong hand of the Government acting in accordance with the orders of the central power of imperial wealth, under the control of the leaders of finance.

"Our top leaders are perfectly aware of the truth. They are presently working at establishing an imperialism of the capital to rule the world. But while they are implementing this plan, they must keep the people busy with political antagonisms.

"We'll therefore speed up the question of reform in the custom rates by the political organization called the Democratic Party; and we'll put the spotlight on the question of protection and of the reciprocity by the Republican Party.

"By dividing the electorate this way, we'll be able to have them spend their energies at struggling amongst themselves on questions that, for us, have no importance whatsoever, and on which we only touch upon as instructors of the common flock.

"It is thus that, through discreet acts, we can maintain what was so generously projected and executed with such a remarkable success."

3. **An 1893 document:** a March 11, 1893 leaflet since then called: "The Panic Circular" addressed by the American Bankers' Association to all national banks throughout the United States:

"The interests of national banks require immediate financial legislation by Congress (the United States Government). Silver, silver certificates, and Treasury bonds (that is to say, all the Government's money) must be retired, and National Bank Notes made the only money.

"This will require the authorization of $500 million to $1 billion of new bonds as the basis of circulation. You will at once retire one-third of your circulation (your paper money) and call in one-half of your loans. Be careful to make a monetary stringency among your patrons, especially among influential businessmen.

"Advocate an extra session of Congress to repeal the purchasing clause of the Sherman Law, and act with other banks of your city in securing a large petition to Congress for its unconditional repeal per accompanying form. Use personal influence with your Congressmen, and particularly let your wishes be known to your senators.

"The future life of national banks, as fixed and safe investments, depends upon immediate action, as there is an increasing sentiment in favor of Government legal-tender notes and silver coinage."

* * *

The well organized Bankers' Association won the day over an ignorant public solely organized for political struggles of colors. A special session of the Congress was convened expressly to demolish the ever-increasing confidence of the people towards a government-issued money.

To force the people and the governments to kneel down in front of the banks, an extreme scarcity of money had to be created. The whole of America felt this scarcity. It was the crisis that was called the "Panic of 1893" planned in the offices of the makers and the destroyers of money, this crisis sowed ruins and pains in every corner of the country.

Louis Even

This article was published in the January-February, 2003 issue of "Michael".

From Debt To Prosperity

25

The Bankers' Manifesto (1892)

The Banker's Manifesto was exposed by US Congress-man Charles A. Lindbergh, SR. (Minnesota), during his term of office (1907-17) as a warning to the citizens of America.

The Father and his famous son, Charles.

— — —

"We (the bankers) must proceed with caution and guard every move made, for the lower order of people are already showing signs of restless commotion. Prudence will there-fore show a policy of apparently yielding to the popular will until our plans are so far consummated that we can declare our designs without fear of any organized resistance.

"The Farmers Alliance and Knights of Labor organiza-tions in the United States should be carefully watched by our trusted men, and we must take immediate steps to con-trol these organizations in our interest or disrupt them.

'Social Credit' Defined   187

"At the coming Omaha Convention to be held July 4th (1892), our men must attend and direct its movement, or else there will be set on foot such antagonism to our designs as may require force to overcome. This at the present time would be premature. We are not yet ready for such a crisis. Capital must protect itself in every possible manner through combination (conspiracy) and legislation.

"The courts must be called to our aid, debts must be collected, bonds and mortgages foreclosed as rapidly as possible.

"When through the process of the law, the common people have lost their homes, they will be more tractable and easily governed through the influence of the strong arm of the government applied to a central power of imperial wealth under the control of the leading financiers. People without homes will not quarrel with their leaders.

"History repeats itself in regular cycles. This truth is well known among our principal men who are engaged in forming an imperialism of the world. While they are doing this, the people must be kept in a state of political antagonism.

"The question of tariff reform must be urged through the organization known as the Democratic Party, and the question of protection with the reciprocity must be forced to view through the Republican Party.

"By thus dividing voters, we can get them to expand their energies in fighting over questions of no importance to us, except as teachers to the common herd. Thus, by discrete action, we can secure all that has been so generously planned and successfully accomplished."

26

A Civilization Of Men Financially Free

by Louis Even

Clifford H. Douglas, the founder of the Social Credit School, was one day asked exactly what he expected the propagation of his doctrine to achieve. The great man answered as follows:

"I will tell you in a broad way what we are aiming at. We are striving to bring to birth a new civilization, something which extends far beyond the bounds of a change in the financial system. We are hoping, by various means, chiefly financial, to enable the human community to step out of one type of civilization into another, and the first requirement, as we see it, is that of absolute economic security."

A liberation:

What will this new civilization be like? How will men in their conduct, in their relationships with one another, be better off than they are today? What will be the special marks of this new civilization in which, according to Douglas, men will be able to build through Social Credit?

No one can give exact and definite answers to such questions. Social Credit has never pretended to blueprint a particular way of life for anyone. It would emancipate man, but it has no wish to dictate to him.

Or, as another Social Credit writer put it, Social Credit is not a panacea, but rather a liberation. A panacea is a universal cure for all diseases, physical or moral. Obviously panaceas have no reality; they are wishful thinking. And Social Credit is certainly not a panacea.

Under a Social Credit system, it will still be necessary to maintain production; there will still be difficulties to surmount, diseases to be cured, sorrows to bear, studies to be pursued, evils to be fought, and virtues to be acquired.

Overweening ambition will have to be restrained, injustices will have to be righted, and charity practiced.

Why then do we speak of a new civilization? Because the men who will build this new civilization and live in it will be men free from the **perpetual anxiety** about tomorrow's bread, just as long as mother nature brings forth enough wheat to supply bread to everyone; and so too for the other material necessities of life.

Today, grain elevators are full to the point of cracking open; farmers lament the ever-increasing surpluses of wheat. Yet for all this, there are many who go hungry.

Under a Social Credit system, such a situation would be impossible. The supply of bread would be determined by the supply of wheat, and not by money. There would be money equivalent to the supply of wheat necessary to make bread; that is to say, there would be both wheat to make bread and money with which to buy bread.

And the same would be true for all the other goods and services available to meet necessities and wants.

The right of all to material goods:

Our present civilization certainly abounds in material and cultural riches. And religion offers its spiritual wealth in abundance. Yet our civilization is a civilization of men in bonds, of men subjected to conditions which more often than not make it difficult or impossible for them to share in these material and cultural treasures.

Even the pursuit of the spiritual is hampered because a man absorbed in the battle for **material necessities** does not live in a climate favorable to the contemplation and acquisition of virtue.

Saint Thomas Aquinas, the great theologian, pointed out the necessity of a certain amount of **material goods** for the practice of virtue. Which is not to say that the mere possession of wealth in itself renders a man virtuous. He must still work at the practice of virtue.

However, the lack of this prerequisite, the want of the **necessary material conditions,** creates an obstacle, and it is the duty of the economic and social order to remove this obstacle. The same holds true for culture.

Earning a livelihood should not so occupy a man that he has no time for other human activities which are more important. But this invariably happens when a man is hemmed in by anxiety for tomorrow's food.

Absolute economic security:

We admit, then, that Douglas is right when he says that, in his mind, the first condition necessary for the foundation of a new and better civilization is "absolute economic security".

"Absolute" — *that is, without conditions.*

In other words, the guarantee of one's daily bread *by the mere fact of one having been born into a world capable of furnishing, quite easily, daily bread to all.*

Relatively few people enjoy such absolute security today.

Even among those who possess the means of making a living for their families, the majority are never sure that they will have these means tomorrow or in ten or twenty years time.

Yet, if our socio-economic system were well ordered, if the acquisition of the goods and products of nature depended only upon the existence in sufficient quantities of such goods, then everyone in Canada, as well as in many other countries, would be able to enjoy absolute economic security.

But when getting hold of goods depends upon financial conditions which are not in accord with the fact of the existence of these goods on the one hand, and of the existence of needs on the other, then absolute economic security is impossible. Security then depends upon fluctuating conditions over which the individual has no control; and any security then degenerates into insecurity.

In physical reality, we have a basis for security; but our financial system is the **root of insecurity.** And since finance is given priority over reality, it follows that insecurity prevails over security.

Hence the statement of Douglas, that the emergence of a new civilization presupposes the application of certain measures, especially in the field of finance. And this is the specific aim of Social Credit's financial propositions which Douglas himself formulated.

What will result?

— But what effects would this absolute economic security have upon individuals? — What effects would it have upon you personally?

Let us suppose that a sum of money, capital, were invested in your name. Let it be that you cannot withdraw the capital thus invested, but that it brings you an annual revenue to the end of your days, sufficient to permit you to live decently and comfortably. This would be for you absolute economic security.

Now, in what way would it affect your life? One thing is sure: you would immediately lose any uncertainty about being able to provide for your needs.

Would you continue to work for a salary? You might, if you liked the work and if the extra revenue permitted you to live a larger and fuller life. Perhaps you would choose to leave this occupation in search for another which, though less lucrative, would be more to your taste (for you now no longer live in the shadow of want).

Perhaps you might choose to work for yourself, profitably or otherwise, making your own free choice of your occupation. You yourself would choose what you wanted to do since you are now, financially, a free man. Your neighbour too would enjoy this privilege, were he to benefit from absolute economic security.

And so too would all citizens when, according to Social Credit principles, all were endowed with this same absolute economic security.

It also becomes apparent at once that certain inevitable changes would take place spontaneously. Since purchasing power would lie, for the most part, in the pockets of the consumers, it would be *they* who would dictate to production what to produce.

The economy would become an economy of the consumer and, in so doing, would regain its true function and end.

Again, the relations between employer and employee

would automatically take on a new aspect. There would no longer be any question of unions of workers and syndicates of employers to fight one another. Men, once assured of their daily bread, would no longer have to submit to the imposition of conditions disagreeable or intolerable.

The various groupings of those engaged in production would almost surely take new forms with the "hired help" assuming the role of **true associates in production.** When men are set free by this economic security, the many pompous dictators will no longer have the power to make them kneel and grovel. Which is perhaps why those who aspire to lord over others are so violently opposed to Social Credit.

The fear of abuse:
— But will there not be those who will abuse this new liberty? Would you yourself abuse it? If you had the chance to acquire this liberty, would you prefer to have it withdrawn for fear you might abuse it?

But let us admit for argument's sake that some might misuse it. Is this a good reason for holding on to an economy of slavery, an economy whose theme is anxiety for the future, when economic security is possible for all?

Pope Pius XI noted that a certain degree of ease and culture does not hinder but rather facilitates the exercise of virtue, providing one makes wise use of such material benefits. He knows very well that some will misuse them. But nevertheless, he claims them for each and everyone as conditions of an economic and social system well and truly constituted. (*Encyclical Quadragesimo Anno.*)

We stated above that, even under a system of absolute economic security, there would still be problems to be resolved. But they will no longer be problems of finance; only such as relate to the functions of man other than economic.

There will be educational, civic, medical, moral, and religious problems — as there are today. But are we afraid of them? Does anyone pretend that the influence of our existing financial system can replace or even aid to any degree the educator, the priest, or help morality and religion?

Why is it that a man should not be able to learn mastery of himself by some other means than that of the continual fear of not having enough to eat? And why should it be necessary for this spirit of fear for tomorrow to be perpetuated through the conniving of the money and credit masters, when our granaries are full to the point of bursting?

The present system is nothing but **economic heresy — want in the presence of abundance.** Social Credit would substitute for it a true orthodox economy, an economy of security for everyone justified by the evidence of concrete, physical facts.

Louis Even

This article was published in the August-September, 2002 issue of "Michael".

From Debt To Prosperity

27

Monetary Power Resides In The Banks

(This modified article, by Louis Even, was first published in the January, 1970 issue of the 'Vers Demain Journal'.)

The **legislative power** has its seat in parliaments, since this is where laws are discussed and voted upon.

The **executive power** resides in the offices of ministers, since it is they — the Prime Minister and his Cabinet — who make the decisions which are carried out by the civil servants.

The **judiciary power** resides in the courts, since that is where the judges practice their duties.

And where does the superpower, the monetary power, reside?

The **monetary power** resides in the banks. It is in the banks that financial credit is actually created and cancelled.

When a bank grants a loan, either to an contractor, a retailer, a consumer, or to a government, new financial credit is created. The banker credits the borrower's account with the granted loan of credit, just as if the borrower had deposited that amount in the bank. But the borrower actually neither brought in nor deposited any money, since he came to the bank to get money he did not have.

The borrower is now able to issue checks on this account that he did not have when he entered the bank, but that he now has upon leaving the bank.

No account of any other customer of the bank was reduced. **This is therefore a new account,** added to the accounts that already exist at the bank. The total credits in the total accounts of the bank are therefore *increased by the amount of this new account.*

There is therefore an *increase in financial credit,* **modern money,** which is put into circulation by the checks the borrower issues on this *new credit.*

On the contrary, when a borrower comes to the bank to repay his **credit** (the loan that had previously been borrowed), it reduces **the amount of credit** in circulation, accordingly. The total **quantity of "blood"** in the economic life is thus reduced by the same amount.

A simple bookkeeping operation, made with one stroke of the **banker's pen,** had created the financial credit. Another simple bookkeeping operation, when the loan was repaid, cancels out and **destroys this credit.**

If, during a given period of time, the **total of the loans** exceeds the **total of the repayments,** this puts more credit into circulation than what is cancelled. On the contrary, if the **total of the repayments** exceeds the **total of the loans,** this causes a reduction of credit from existing circulation.

If the period of reduction persists, the whole economic body is affected by it — **it is called a crisis** — a crisis caused by a restriction of credit and its flow.

Since the borrower must pay back **more** than what he borrowed, because of the interest, he must **withdraw from circulation** more money than what was put into circulation.

For this, he must **withdraw from circulation** more money that has been put there by other borrowers.

As every **new amount of credit** comes from the banks, under the condition of paying back more money *than the capital amounts loaned out,* **other people must also borrow,** following the first borrowers. The latter have **even more difficulties** in repaying their loans, since they have to take more money out of the credit in circulation, which is already reduced by the amount of money that the first borrower had to repay in interest.

This chain goes on, in the same way, for the next borrowers, and eventually, **some borrows can never pay back their loans!** Then the banks restrict *further* loans, which slows down the whole economic life. **But the banks blame this situation on the population that suffers from it in the end.**

In order to have the flow of credit that is required for economic life resume, a chain of new loans will have to take place again, breeding a bigger and bigger chain of debts.

A tool of the superpower:

The present banking system is the tool used by the monetary superpower to maintain its supremacy over their governments and nations. The banks are supported in all this by the ridiculous, *politico-financial* rule that binds the distribution of purchasing power to employment, in a production cause that requires fewer and fewer employees to supply the goods necessary for life.

Do not conclude from this that your local banker is part of this dictatorship. He is only a subordinate who, most likely, is not even aware that when he inscribes loans in the ledgers of his bank, he creates credit, and that the repayments inscribed in his ledger destroy, cancel, this credit.

It is not him who dictates the restrictions of credit that make the economic body anemic. He only acts upon the orders that he receives, without thinking or worrying about the consequences.

You may still hear backward scholars **deny that the volume of credit in circulation** depends upon the action of the banks. These backward scholars, who resist the obvious, are an invaluable support to the superpower, through their **ignorance** — if it is really ignorance on their part, or through **vested interests** that bind them, or through their **collusion with a power** which can bring them easy promotions and rewards.

Upper-class bankers, on the other hand, know very well that **financial credit,** which makes up the bulk of modern money, **is created and cancelled in the ledgers of banks.**

A distinguished British banker — the Right Honorable Reginald McKenna, one-time British Chancellor of the Exchequer, and Chairman of the Midland Bank, one of the Big Five (five largest banks of England) — addressed an annual general meeting of the shareholders of the bank, on January 25, 1924, and said (as recorded in his book, *Post-War Banking*):

"I am afraid the ordinary citizen will not like to be told that the banks can, and do, create and destroy money. The amount of finance in existence varies only with the action of the banks in increasing or decreasing deposits and bank purchases. We know how this is effected. **Every loan, overdraft, or bank purchase creates a deposit, and every repayment of**

a loan, overdraft, or bank sale destroys a deposit."

Having also been Minister of Finance, McKenna knew very well where the bigger of the **two powers** — the **power of the banks,** and the **power of the sovereign government of the country** — resided. And he was frank enough to state the following, which is very uncommon among bankers of his official level:

"They (the banks) control the credit of the nation, direct the policies of governments, and keep in the palm of their hands the destinies of the peoples."

This is a statement which is in complete agreement with what Pope Pius XI wrote in his Encyclical Letter *Quadragesimo Anno,* in 1931:

"Those who, because they hold and control money, are able also to govern credit and determine its allotment, for that reason supplying, so to speak, the lifeblood to the entire economic body, and grasping, as it were, in their hands the very soul of production, so that no one dare breathe against their will."

From Debt To Prosperity

Today's financial system is not adapted to progress

It paralyzes the whole economic system

In dribs and drabs for peace, buckets of money for war

28
The Aim Of The Financiers

The Financiers believe that they are the only ones capable of governing mankind properly, and in order to be able to impose their will upon every individual and control the whole world, they invented the present debt-based money system.

They want to bring every nation in the world to such a state of crisis that these countries will think that they have no alternative but to accept the miracle solution of the Financiers to save them from disaster:

Complete centralization, a single world currency, and a one-world government, in which all nations will be abolished, or forced to give-up their sovereignty.

To consolidate their power, the Financiers also want to eliminate every existing national currency, and to install a one-world currency.

In the 1970s, Dr. Hanrick Eldeman, Chief Analyst of the Common Market Confederacy in Brussels, unveiled a plan to "straighten out world chaos": a three-story tall computer located in the administration building of the headquarters of the Common Market, in Brussels, Belgium.

People who work there call it "the Beast". The plan implies a system of digital enumeration of each human being on earth. Thus the computer would give each inhabitant of the world a number to be used for each purchase or sale.

This number would be invisibly tattooed by laser (or implanted with a microchip) either on the forehead or on the back of the hand. This would establish a **walking credit card system**. And the number could be seen only through infrared scanners, installed in special verification counters or in business places.

Dr. Eldeman pointed out that by using **three entries of six digits each** — eighteen digits in all — every inhabitant of the world would be given a distinct credit card number.

This reminds us strangely of what the Apostle John wrote in the Book of Revelation (13: 16-18) regarding the prophecy of Jesus Christ:

> "And he (the Beast) shall make all, both little and great, rich and poor, freemen and slaves, to receive a mark on their right hands, or on their foreheads, and that none might buy or sell, unless he carried this mark, which was the beast's name, or the number that stands for his name. Here is wisdom; he that has understanding, let him count the number of the beast. For it is the number of a man: and the number of him is six hundred and sixty-six."

The avowed goal of the banks is to eliminate all cash and to force people to use debit cards as the only means of payment for their needs.

A few decades ago, before the invention of computers and microchips, such a system would have seemed far-fetched, a product of science fiction. But now everyone knows about the existence of debit cards with which you can buy anything in stores without the need to carry any cash on you, the amount of your purchase being debited automatically from your bank account. The avowed goal of the banks is to eliminate all cash, and to force people to use debit cards as the only means of payment.

There is always the risk of losing one's debit card, or of having somebody else illegally use it. So here comes the ultimate solution: to link people personally to their card, so there is no way they can lose it or have it stolen! And there you have it: a micro-computer chip can be implanted under your skin, or a **three six-digital mark** can be tattooed on your skin... just as described in the bible Revelation of Saint John.

Everything will be in place for a government that wants to control everybody's move, since they will know everything about you: all that you buy, where and when you buy it, who you phone, how much money you have, will all be inscribed on this card. And if, for whatever reason, you are classified as an "undesirable person" or as an "enemy of the State" by the government, they will only have to erase your number from the central computer, and you will no longer be able to buy and sell (and thus be condemned to disappear before long).

The prayers and sacrifices to obtain the assistance of Heaven are certainly necessary to thwart the plan of the Financiers. But a technique — a temporal means — is also necessary to thwart the plan of the Financiers: — the Social Credit Reform, conceived by the Scottish engineer, Clifford Hugh Douglas; the only Reform that the Financiers really fear, that would put an end to their power to control the nations.

"Social Credit" means money created by society without debt, issued with new production, and withdrawn from circulation as production is consumed — instead of having a banking credit as it is the case today —money created as a debt by private banks.

Douglas first thought that once his discovery and its implications would be brought to the attention of the governments and of those in charge of the economy, they would hasten to implement it.

But Douglas soon made another discovery: the Financiers who ruled the economy were not interested in changing the financial system and its flaws and consequences. Wars, waste, poverty, social friction, etc. are what they desire and even deliberately foster, in order to impose their solution of a one-world government on the nations of the world.

So the Financiers did everything they could to stop and silence the Social Credit idea by a conspiracy of silence in the news media, or deliberate falsification of Douglas's doctrine, in order to render it vulnerable; by calumnies and ridicule against the apostles of "Michael".

Douglas wrote in his book *Warning Democracy:*

"So rapid was the progress made by the Social Credit ideas between 1919 and 1923, both in this country (Great Britain) and abroad, and so constantly did ideas derived from them appear in the pages of the press, that the interests threatened by them became alarmed, and took what were, on the whole, effective steps to curtail their publicity.

"In this country the Institute of Bankers allocated five million pounds (then the equivalent of $24 million dollars) to combat the 'subversive' ideas of ourselves and other misguided people who wished to tinker with the financial system.

"The large Press Associations were expressly instructed that my own name should not be mentioned in the public press, **and no metropolitan newspaper in this country or the United States was allowed to give publicity, either to correspondence or to contributions bearing upon the subject.**

"In spite of this the Canadian Parliamentary Inquiry at which I was a witness (in 1923) managed to expose on the one hand the ignorance of even leading bankers of the fundamental problems with which they had to deal, and on the other hand the lengths to which the financial power was prepared to go to retain control of the situation."

The best way that the Financiers found to stop the advancement of the Social Credit idea was the creation of political parties falsely bearing the name "Social Credit", to make people think that voting for a new party is sufficient to change the system.

What is needed is the education of the people, to force the elected representatives to serve the population itself, instead of serving the Financiers.

Fortunately, all the so-called "Social Credit parties" are dead and buried now, but they did a lot of damage and spread confusion in the minds of the people while they existed.

Douglas predicted that the present debt-money system of the Bankers would become unworkable and fall by itself, because of all of the unpayable debts that it creates.

All the countries in the world are struggling with skyrocketing debts and heading for disaster, even though everybody knows these debts can never be paid off. Other factors announce the inevitable fall of the present system: automation, for example, which makes full employment impossible.

Douglas said that **"a psychological moment"** will come, a moment of **critical mass** when the population, given the gravity of the situation, and despite all the power of the Financiers, will have suffered their debt-money system long enough, and will be disposed to study and accept Social Credit.

Douglas wrote the following in 1924, in his book *Social Credit:*

> "The position will be tremendous in its importance.
>
> "A comparatively short period will probably serve to decide whether we are to master the mighty economic and social machine that we have created, or whether it is to master us; and during that period a small impetus from a body of men who know what to do and how to do it, may make the difference between yet one more retreat into the Dark Ages, or the emergence into the full light of a day of such splendor as we can at present only envisage dimly.
>
> "It is this necessity for the recognition of the psychological moment, and the fitting to that moment of appropriate action, which should be present in the minds of that small minority which is seized of the gravity of the present times."

Louis Even, at the end of an article written in 1970 and entitled *"Social Credit, yes — Party, no"*, repeated this idea of Douglas:

"The Social Creditors of the Michael Journal maintain, along with Douglas, that as regards Social Credit, the most effective work to do is to enlighten the population on the monopoly of financial credit, attributing to it the bad fruits of which it is the cause in the lives of people, of families, of institutions; and, in front of these bad fruits, to expose the doctrine of genuine Social Credit, which is so brilliant and in keeping with common sense.

"They also endeavor to develop within themselves, and to also radiate, a Social Credit spirit, which is clearly in keeping with the spirit of the Gospel: a spirit of service and not of domination, not of an insatiable pursuit of money or material goods, which is of the same nature — with a less powerful means — as the spirit of the barons of High Finance.

"Whether the collapse of the present financial system, under the weight of its own enormities, or events that have been foretold many times by privileged souls — events one certainly cannot doubt of when one sees the present decadence of moral standards, apostasy, the paganization of affluent nations that used to be Christian — occur soon, in either case, the living or the survivors of those events won't be without a light to establish a social economic system worthy of its name."

The point to remember in all of this is that the present financial system, which creates money as a debt, is the main means of the Financiers to establish a one-world government. Debt finance is the bridge that leads us from a free society to complete dictatorship.

And the only thing the Financiers fear, the only thing that can stop them in their plan of world conquest, is the reform of the present financial system, the establishment of an honest debt-free money system, along the lines of the Social Credit philosophy — when one realizes the importance of the Social Credit Solution, and the importance of spreading it and making it known.

This is why Soviet Foreign Minister Molotov had said to Dr. Hewlett Johnson, Archbishop of Canterbury, in the 30's:

"We know all about Social Credit. It is the one theory in the world we fear."

Subscribe to the *Michael* Journal
Published by the Pilgrims of St. Michael

Michael is a journal of ideas, independent of any political party, and free from any tie. It refuses any paid advertisement, and lives only from its subscriptions.

Michael is the voice of the people; to make governments serve the people.

Michael scorns a scarce economy, and the bankers' debt-money system. It advocates the new economics, *Social Credit,* an economy of plenty and freedom for all. Poverty amidst plenty is *nonsense.*

Help them by sending $20.00, and you will receive the *Michael* Journal every two months, for the next two years.

Send your check or money order to:

**Michael Journal
1101 Principale St.
Rougemont, Que.
Canada — J0L 1M0**

From Debt To Prosperity

The abundance of goods distributed to all. Money problems solved.

The book, *In This Age Of Plenty,* presents a new conception of finance of the money system that would definitely free society form purely financial problems.

Its author, Louis Even, sets out the outlines of the Social Credit financial proposals, conceived by the Scottish engineer Clifford Hugh Douglas.

Today, when there is no money, municipalities lay aside urgent works, requested by the population, undone, even though there is everything needed — men and materials — to carry out all of these works.

Social Credit would change all of this. It would make money a simple servant, a mere bookkeeping system, but a just one, in keeping with existing conditions. Money would come into being as production is made, and money would disappear as production disappears.

Today, the production system does not distribute purchasing power to every one. It distributes it only to those who are employed in production. And the more the production comes form the machine, the less it comes from human labor. Production even increases, whereas required employment decreases. So there is a conflict between progress, which eliminates the need for human labor, and the system, which distributes purchasing power only to the employed.

Yet, everyone has the right to live, even those who are not employed. This is why, without in any way disturbing the system of reward for work, Social Credit would distribute to every individual a periodical income, called a "social dividend". This dividend would allow everyone to enjoy the fruits of progress.

And they hesitate to change the wheel!

The dictatorship of the bankers and their debt-money system are not limited to one country, but exist in every country in the world. They are working to keep their control tight, since one country freeing itself from this dictatorship and issuing its own *interest- and debt-free currency,* setting the example of what an honest system could be, would be enough to bring about the worldwide collapse of the bankers' swindling debt-money system.

From Debt To Prosperity

"For we wrestle not against flesh and blood, but against principalities, against powers, against the rulers of the darkness of this world, against spiritual wickedness in high places.

"Wherefore take unto you the whole armour of God, that ye may be able to withstand in the evil day, and having done all, to stand."

— Ephesians 6:12-13.

Give Yourself Credit: *Money Doesn't Grow On Trees*
http://tinyurl.com/39eoywm

My Home Is My Castle: *Beware Of The Dog*
http://tinyurl.com/37wk48v

From Debt To Prosperity

Commercial Redemption: *The Hidden Truth*
http://tinyurl.com/37tdbrf

Hardcore Redemption-In-Law: *Commercial Freedom And Release*
http://tinyurl.com/2ul4t5e

Oil Beneath Our Feet: *America's Energy Non-Crisis*
http://tinyurl.com/34dhbur

Untold History Of America: *Let The Truth Be Told*
http://tinyurl.com/36tkc9q

New Beginning Study Course: *Connect The Dots And See*
http://tinyurl.com/37n8cyj

Monitions of a Mountain Man: *Manna, Money, & Me*
http://tinyurl.com/377l66n

Maine Street Miracle: *Saving Yourself And America*
http://tinyurl.com/38lk966

Reclaim Your Sovereignty: *Take Back Your Christian Name*
http://tinyurl.com/392kzqr

Epistle to the Americans I: *What you don't know about The Income Tax*
http://tinyurl.com/3yz8mun

Epistle to the Americans II: *What you don't know about American History*
http://tinyurl.com/33cawzr

Epistle to the Americans III: *What you don't know about Money*
http://tinyurl.com/3az8r7w

www.ingramcontent.com/pod-product-compliance
Lightning Source LLC
Chambersburg PA
CBHW062142280526
45788CB00001B/269